LEAVES OF GRASS
One Hundred Years After

LEAVES OF GRASS
One Hundred Years After

Essays by

WILLIAM CARLOS WILLIAMS, RICHARD CHASE
LESLIE A. FIEDLER, KENNETH BURKE
DAVID DAICHES, AND J. MIDDLETON MURRY

Edited and with an Introduction by
MILTON HINDUS

STANFORD UNIVERSITY PRESS
STANFORD, CALIFORNIA

LONDON: OXFORD UNIVERSITY PRESS

Stanford University Press
Stanford, California
Copyright 1955 by the Board of Trustees of the
Leland Stanford Junior University
Printed in the United States of America
Original edition 1955
Reprinted 1966

The Editor dedicates this book to

MAURICE ZOLOTOW

for his sustained and sustaining faith

Contents

LEAVES OF GRASS
One Hundred Years After

"Let America, then, prize and cherish her writers; yea let her glorify them. They are not so many in number as to exhaust her goodwill. And while she has good kith and kin of her own to take to her bosom, let her not lavish her embraces upon the household of an alien. . . . Even if there were no strong literary individualities among us, nevertheless let America first praise mediocrity even, in her children, before she praises (for everywhere merit demands acknowledgment from everyone) the best excellence in the children of any other land. . . . It is not meant that all American writers should studiously cleave to nationality in their writings; only this, no American writer should write like an Englishman or a Frenchman; let him write like a man, for then he will be sure to write like an American. . . . Let us boldly condemn all imitation though it comes to us graceful and fragrant as the morning; and foster all originality, though at first it be crabbed and ugly as our own pine knots. . . . The truth is, that in one point of view this matter of a national literature has come to such a pass with us, that in some sense we must turn bullies, else the day is lost. . . ."

MELVILLE, *Hawthorne and His Mosses*

MILTON HINDUS

The Centenary of *Leaves of Grass*

THE IDEA of celebrating the centenary of a man's work rather than that of his birth or death although not unprecedented (the centenaries of Melville's *Moby Dick* and of Thoreau's *Walden* having been observed in recent years), is still unusual enough possibly to deserve some notice. Its excuse, like that of all celebrations, is love, which seeks occasions on which to express itself and, finding none, invents them. An opportunity, once sought, is readily discovered. In his essay *A Backward Glance o'er Travel'd Roads* Whitman had said of his lifework: "The volume is a sortie—whether to prove triumphant, and conquer its field of aim and escape and construction, nothing less than a hundred years from now can fully answer." Since these words were set down in 1888, it is still somewhat early for any final judgments according to the criterion indicated, but the year 1955 which marks the initial century of the survival of *Leaves of Grass* seems to present an excellent excuse for a fresh stocktaking.

The most unambiguous answer to the question of Whitman came in the letter with which William Carlos Williams accompanied the manuscript of his essay: "Thank you for the opportunity to have contributed to the celebration over the centenary of the publication of Whitman's *Leaves of Grass*, a book as important as we are likely to see in the next thousand years, especially a book written by an American." If our project had done no more than inspire this single sentiment on the part of Dr. Williams, it would, I think, have justified itself.

It has, as a matter of fact, done much more. Richard Chase and Leslie Fiedler have been impelled to contribute (each in a different way—one through a history of the poet's life, the other through that of his reputation) a restoration of Whitman's original intentions to us. We have an attempt here to interpret the poet in such a way that his work may become viable once more to the sensibilities of a ruthlessly critical generation. Fiedler's essay in particular is notable for its pres-

3

entation of the bard not unintentionally involved in a heroic comedy of errors, of mistaken identities and intentions misunderstood. At the end we are left with the hypothesis that Whitman may have been "simply" a writer—that is to say, one who, though willing enough to *represent*, may have had to content himself with being interesting enough to read. This latter ambition he fulfilled by imparting that unique verve to his language, which in the end is the only guaranty of a writer's survival.

The merit of Kenneth Burke's criticism seems to be in his ability, even when he is most far-fetched in his analyses, to return our attention to the particular words which Whitman uses—because it is in the particularities of his language that the poet's message must be communicated. The search for subtleties of intertwined meanings (many of them below the threshold of consciousness) may degenerate sometimes into a purposeless wandering among distracting flyspecks. The critic steers his delicate craft by the twin warning lights of Whitman and Mallarmé. Whitman's assurance that the *words* of his poems are "nothing—the drift of them everything" is matched on the opposite side by Mallarmé's insistence to Degas that "poems are not made out of ideas but out of words!" The reader perceives how these paradoxical half-truths (designed to catch our attention through the brilliant excess in their expression) complement each other, and he conducts his way at a safe distance between them both. It deserves to be noted, too, that the needs of an illuminated criticism in relation to a writer's work change with the passing of time. What is not obvious enough to one generation becomes too obvious for another generation. As hints to a potential audience at a time when neither of them was widely understood, Mallarmé's and Whitman's cautions as to how their works were to be read were no doubt necessary for self-preservation. But now that they have received their fair share of warmth and appreciation from the world, it may be refreshing to reverse the application of their critical formulas, to judge Whitman by the standards suggested by Mallarmé and Mallarmé by those of Whitman. What, if anything, is left of Whitman's work if we choose to ignore his general "drift"* of

---

* One interpretation of the word "drift," of course, would bring Whitman and Mallarmé much closer together. That is the meaning of *drift* as an accumulation, a mass, a piling-up—as in the word snow*drift*. According to this interpretation, Whitman would not be denying the importance of his words but of *his words taken separately from each other*. The effect of the snowfall is not to be felt in the individual flake but in the grandeur and magnitude of the "drift." *Drift* may also be interpreted plausibly in a verbal manner as referring to the propulsive rhythms which inform Whitman's lines and which are perhaps the principal cause

meaning and attend to the precise terms in which he stated it? On the other hand, what is Mallarmé worth if we resist the hypnosis of his phraseology and approach his work from the side of his abstract ideas? Will the verse of each of these poets be found to retain its hard integrity under these less tolerant forms of examination? What Burke seems to me to have done is to perform an *experiment* to find the answer, in the case of Whitman—an experiment the results of which the interested reader may wish to check against those obtained in Randall Jarrell's similarly motivated, earlier essay which he called: "Some Lines from Whitman."

David Daiches and John Middleton Murry use an approach to Whitman which is more traditional. At any rate, its postulates seem much more familiar to readers of Whitman criticism over the past century. The personal modifications of the tradition which they make are the result of their special qualities of sensitivity. I have never read anything by Mr. Murry—whether on Dostoevski, Shakespeare, Keats, Swift, or the other masters upon whom he has spent his really Protean gifts of critical sympathy—without learning to view the writer considered in a revelatory new light. It is to an exciting journey among masterpieces that he always invites us. He seems to me to possess the great talent (there is perhaps none more important to the critic) of being able to subordinate himself entirely to the object of his aesthetic concern until, in the words with which Marcel Proust once described an interpreter of a piece of music, "himself one no longer sees, and he is nothing now but a window opening out upon a great work of art." It is a feeling of humility and of self-denying identification with another person (more and more infrequently to be found among contemporary critics) to which the greatest tribute may have been spoken by Whitman himself when he remarked of someone to his friend and biographer, Horace Traubel: "He has enthusiasm: without that, what is a man?"

In this symposium on Whitman's life and work, the banalities of indiscriminate praise or blame find scant refuge. The critics go off in as many directions as the poetry or facts invite them; they digress, hesitate, qualify, disagree with each other and occasionally with themselves. The results of their intensive cerebration and sympathies do not lend themselves to any neat organization or unquestionable conclusions (is there any writer to whom such conclusions are more alien and inapplicable than they are to Whitman?). If the purpose of a book

---

of their felt power. Yet it is clear to me that, in using the word "drift," Whitman was primarily referring to something abstract rather than concrete, something much closer to the meaning: "tendency of an argument; purport; aim."

of criticism is not to become an end in itself or to replace the literary experience it presumably is devoted to, but by a certain "radioactivity" of ideas and suggestions to send us back to look at the original work with an alertness of attention we have not known before, then I hope it may be said that my labors as an editor have not been unfruitful.

II

The contradictions of his critics have something in common with the contradictions of Whitman himself. Everyone, of course, quotes his well-known lines:

Do I contradict myself?
Very well then I contradict myself,
(I am large, I contain multitudes.)

But this is unfortunately where the matter is allowed to end instead of only beginning (unless it is to cite the passages which demonstrate that Whitman's complacency in the face of contradiction goes back to that of his master Emerson). Instead of exploring some of the contradictions (which, after all, are not so obvious to the naked eye as to need no tracing), the attempt is usually made too soon to extract a specious form of unity out of the "multitudes" of his diversity, and to yoke together by what seems to be main force concepts which, if we believe him, nature has put so far asunder. Instead of using this rough-and-ready method (which insults its subject by assuming that Whitman could not think as well as his critics and that his words were a mere matter of hit or miss), it should be interesting to chart a few of what may be called the Antinomies of Whitman. These striking Antinomies seem to me to be grounded not on the carelessness or whimsicality of the poet's thought but on the deep-lying limitations on the province of the human reason itself. They should *not*, in other words, be either idly dismissed or glibly accepted, and, in either case, should not be judged as trivial and unimportant.

Whitman sometimes presents himself and is often presented to us by his followers as one for whom there existed no difference at all between literature and life. The classic expression of this view is contained in the line: "Who touches this book touches a man." This striking sentiment, however, seems to be directly at odds with the one he confided to Traubel when he said that *Leaves of Grass* was only "a language experiment." While the former statement impressed his earlier critics, the latter is catching the attention of his more recent ones (for example, Matthiessen in his *American Renaissance* and perhaps, by implication, Leslie Fiedler in our own volume). Our critics are interested in the language experimenter because he must be a conscious artist as contrasted with a spontaneous one. They are no longer content to see in art merely a naïve reflection of reality, still less reality itself unretouched. Art has come to be for them, more and more, reality as it is refracted through the medium of recalcitrant words. Art, if it is not the contrary of reality, is in an oblique or indirect relation to it.

There is no doubt that Whitman more often than not encouraged his readers to forget the difference between literature and life and, therefore, was at least partly responsible for such misunderstandings as Mrs. Gilchrist's, who interpreted his verse as a personal invitation to come to Philadelphia and marry the poet. (Traubel tells the story of another poor woman who wrote to Whitman, putting herself at his disposal that they might conceive a child together "on a mountain top." Whitman wrote on the envelope of her letter: "Insane asylum?" Whereupon even the faithful Traubel was moved to ask him if he had ever read his own work!)

Corresponding to his denial of the boundaries between art and life, there is a tendency on the part of Whitman to slight his music in favor of his message. To W. R. Thayer he said: "I don't value the poetry in what I have written as much as the teaching; the poetry is only a horse for the other to ride." This may help account for the fact that his Pegasus has so uneven a gait as to throw many of his riders at the beginning of the course. Whitman rebelled against the demands of his fellow craftsmen: "The trouble is that writers are too literary—too damned literary . . . art for art's sake: think of it . . . Let a man really accept that—let that be his ruling thought—and he is lost . . . Instead of regarding literature as only an instrument in the service of something larger than itself, it looks upon itself as an end—as a fact to be finally worshipped, adored. To me that's all a horrible blasphemy, a bad-smelling apostasy." And in the same vein he wrote in *A Backward Glance*: "No one will get at my verses who insists upon viewing them as a literary performance, or as aiming mainly toward art or aestheticism."

On the other hand, what could be more purely aesthetic or antididactic than his statement to Traubel: "I approach nature not to explain but to picture. Who can explain?" Or take the contradictions with reference to his technique of composition. He strove ceaselessly for the effect of improvisation in his verse and achieved the illusion of spontaneity so successfully that his followers, in imitating him, wrote "free verse" (of which he never dreamed) and were not content till they had loosened all bonds of rule and order. Yet he had insisted that "writers should school themselves," and said that "my own defect is more in the direction of interpolation, interlineation—in the insertion of words. I am only slowly satisfied with my verbal achievements: I remake over and over, as you have seen." And one who has looked over some of his tortured manuscripts must agree that this was so.

Who but a conscious artist, "a language experimenter," could have written such very different variations on the same theme as "O Captain! My Captain!" and "When Lilacs Last in the Dooryard Bloom'd"? Or have undertaken to transpose the prose Preface to the edition of '55 into the poem *By Blue Ontario's Shore*? It is true that he wasn't capable very often of improving upon his original and sometimes actually spoiled his initial effect. Given time, he tended to "overcook" his poems, but he was not inclined to make a virtue of necessity, and whatever he might say about the delights of "loafing" he never seemed to be lazy about trying to improve himself as an artist.

Those who encapsulate for us a little gospel according to Whitman were repudiated by him in advance. He said to Traubel: "I for my own account find any unqualified dogmatic generalizations offensive: just as much so—maybe more so—in my friends than in my enemies." This is only another way of putting the idea which he had already included in his poem "Whoever You Are Holding Me Now in Hand": "Even while you should think you had unquestionably caught me, behold! / Already you see I have escaped from you."

But this conclusion warning against conclusions may be confronted with statements to a different effect, as when he said to Traubel: "I don't think there can be any great character, really great character, without centrality—some prevailing idea, some purpose at heart: more and more that conviction possesses me, absorbs me." One might turn this reflection upon Whitman himself and say that his antinomies prove that he was not a great character, a "really great character." I myself do not believe the answer is so simple.

Whitman was not merely the destroyer of old principles of poetic organization but was actively in search of new ones, which he imperfectly apprehended. The search is implied by his contrast between the poems of the past, which he said resembled the pillars of the Parthenon, and those of the future, which would be like the waves of the sea. Though the figure of speech contains a great difficulty at its heart, because the architectural construction is man-made while the work of nature is not, it is important to notice the implication that the poetry of the future will be governed by law just as the poetry of the past has been, though the laws may be very different from each other.

The comparison of his new principles of metrical organization with those of certain portions of the Bible is first suggested by Whitman himself. In the Preface to *Leaves of Grass*, he had referred to the American poem which he was projecting there as "the great psalm of the republic." And when he says in *Salut au Monde!* "I hear the Hebrew reading his records and psalms," that is perhaps to be taken literally; it is quite possible that Whitman's all-embracing curiosity brought him, like the composer Wagner, into the synagogue where he could hear the psalms being chanted in their original tongue. It is a fact that David's Psalms are as unruly as Whitman's, and that after three thousand years of study they have never been successfully reduced to a fixed pattern, though the ear convinces us, in the one case as in the other, that some kind of form, of a very eccentric kind it may be, has been impressed upon the words. When Whitman inveighed against formalism in literature ("The literary formalists, even the gifted ones, go to pieces somewhere almost inevitably before they finish a job"), it is important to realize that in his own mind he is talking not against the necessity of form of some kind but only against such narrow interpreters of form as would compel him to squeeze himself into a Procrustean bed that would surely have resulted in crippling his inspiration.

I myself perceive two things clearly within his work. The first is the *flash* of revelation in the individual phrase and word: "the Union always surrounded by *blatherers* and always calm and impregnable" or "Faith is the *antiseptic* of the soul," where the energy of the phrase is concentrated in a single word, usually of modern invention and connotations: "blatherers," "antiseptic." The second is the propulsive rhythm which is indefinable but which underlies all of his verse and much of his prose. It is present to the ear if not to the analytical intelligence; it can be demonstrated by reading aloud though it cannot be described. It accounts for the feeling even of his worst foes that he is *something* of a genius.

After all the efforts that have been made during the last century to catch his haunting, nameless tune, it should be admitted that "free verse" (to adopt this barbarous nomenclature for a moment) is not the easiest form of poetry to write (as all freshmen think) but the hardest, for in this form the poet's soul stands forth, minus all dodges, disguises, and mere cleverness—"bare and naked, trembling at itself."

The contradictions of Whitman, which he was aware of but could not or did not care to iron out, may have been caused by the conflict between his conscious mind and his unconscious one. It was not easy for him always to harness his *team* of Pegasuses together. The poet's unconscious mind often shows an almost studied contempt for his conscious one, even as a great composer (like Handel) may ignore completely the verbal quality of the text to which he has chosen to set his compelling music. There is a measure of bravado in his doing this. The composer knows that his music can lift up to the heavens the deadest words, and the poet is aware that no matter how confused or inadequate his ideas are his passion will carry all before him. In this connection, Whitman said to Traubel: "While I am willing to accord Goethe a very high place, I could not accord him the highest: the highest place would seem to demand first of all passion, warmth—not artistic power, deftness of technique, primarily, but human passion."

Paul Valéry says that poetry is composed of "strange words which seem created by *another* person than him who speaks them and addressed to *another* than him who hears them . . . a language within a language." The formulation seems to evoke the truth of our actual experience. Poetry appears to be a secret language—a sort of illicit communication between the unconscious of the writer and the unconscious of the reader, a momentary escape for both from the area of prosaic responsibility. Neither one really knows what he is doing or can be held accountable for that spellbound or hypnotic state of mind.

The reasons for which readers have been affected by Whitman's poems are doubtful, but the depth and overwhelming nature of the effect itself cannot be doubted. They talk about him like men possessed, just as did the rhapsode Ion when he talked of Homer to Socrates twenty-five hundred years ago. This becomes especially noticeable when the speakers are Englishmen, who are by habit and tradition given to understatement. Robert Louis Stevenson said that *Leaves of Grass* "tumbled the world upside down" for him, and John Addington Symonds said it had affected him more than any book save the Bible.

From the beginning, Whitman had been compensated for the smallness of his audience by the intensity of its devotion to him. Valéry speaks of what he terms "the iron law of literature—that what is valid for one alone is worth nothing." Art cannot be merely a solipsistic exercise. Valéry's formula, in spite of the novelty of its metaphorical garb, is one of the classical truths of criticism. It may be found in other forms, in Samuel Johnson and in the philosopher David Hume. Johnson cites, as the highest testimony to the power of Shakespeare, the fact that his work has been transmitted from generation to generation, gaining "new honors at every transmission," while Hume proves to his own satisfaction that Homer must be a classic by the pragmatic observation that his work is held in as much esteem in modern London and Paris as it was held in ancient Rome and Athens.

It should be noted, however, that while Valéry, like his eighteenth-century predecessors, demands communicability from the artist to his audience, a work of art may be perfectly valid though it affect at the start only one enthusiast. With Whitman's work, this statement touches on a recurrent problem. Bliss Perry, in his book on Whitman, has justly remarked: "Numbers count for nothing, when one is reckoning the audience of a poet." A similar sentiment, with a new twist to it, is given by Traubel when he recalls that Felix Adler, the father of Ethical Culture in America and one of Whitman's admirers, said to him that readers must not only be counted—they must be weighed.

But what is the weight of a reader? One passionate convert to a cause has sometimes proselytized innumerable others. Is that what is meant by a weighty reader? Appreciation of art is at least partly a social matter. Attitudes of other people affect our own attitudes, no matter how much we may take pride in our independence of taste. And undoubtedly the attitudes of some people—those who speak with seeming authority in contrast with those who are merely guessing—are more infectious than those of others. (In passing, we may remark how much easier a task it is in art to communicate a distaste for something than it is to plant and to cultivate a taste. The destructive critics outnumber the creative ones and have much the easier job of it.)

What Whitman can do for some of his readers is indicated in the letter with which Emerson in 1855 acknowledged receipt of the strange new book. "It has the best merits, namely, of fortifying and encouraging." It was Whitman's own ambition to be measured by such a criterion. In *Democratic Vistas* he quoted with approval a passage from a paper recently delivered by the Librarian of Congress: "The true question to ask respecting a book is *has it helped any human soul?*" And in *A Backward Glance* he clings to the same standard of judgment: "I say the profoundest service that poems or other writings can do for their reader is not merely to satisfy the intellect, or supply something polish'd and arresting, nor even to depict great passions, or persons or events, but to fill him with vigorous and clean manliness, religiousness, and give him *good heart* as a radical possession and habit."

Most readers unfortunately get out of a book no more than they have put into it—which is little enough. "We receive but what we give," as Coleridge told Wordsworth. The hollowness of heart which Whitman complained of in *Democratic Vistas* has become something worse in the wasteland of T. S. Eliot. In a world of hollow men Whitman's reputation cannot be high, for the very conditions which make us need his message militate against the possibility of its being found. Schopenhauer said that when a book and a head meet and one of them sounds empty, it may not always be the book. Whitman delivered himself of a thought similar to this: "Not the book needs so much to be the complete thing, but the reader of the book does." The paradox is that those who are complete in themselves are not likely to be in search of illumination in a writer, while those who are defective in some way are not likely to succeed in their search.

Robert Louis Stevenson must have foreseen the dilemma when he qualified the most extravagant recommendation of *Leaves of Grass* with the statement: "But it is only a book for those who have the gift of reading." What is *the gift of reading*? Whitman himself may have supplied the hint when he wrote that "He who walks a furlong without sympathy walks to his own funeral dressed in his shroud." The ideal reader, too, it seems should be filled with sympathy and be possessed of a plasticity of feeling capable of taking the most diverse, even contradictory, shapes at the bidding of a proper writer. Stevenson himself was every writer's dream of a reader—one having a limitless, Gargantuan appetite and tolerance for the most different kinds of fare. He was able not only to swallow Whitman whole, but—what was perhaps an even more difficult feat for an Englishman of his generation—Dostoevski as well. He repressed his prejudices completely and consulted only his taste. A reader of a completely opposite kind was Henry James. Though, as we learn from the reminiscences of Edith Wharton in *A Backward Glance*, he came to feel Whitman very deeply and to regard him as the greatest of American poets, this was not a natural, spontaneous taste with him as it was with Stevenson but a slowly acquired and cultivated one—everything had to be cultivated in the case of James—and his first impulse (the same was true of his reactions to Dostoevski and Baudelaire) was to reject him out of hand. James, as a young man just out of college, had written a review of *Drum-Taps* which, along with Swinburne's essay *Whitmania*, has the dubious distinction of rating as one of the most ferocious of attempted demolitions of this indestructible poet.

Nietzsche in *Thus Spake Zarathustra* has put down a sobering thought for all readers of books: "Es ist nicht leicht möglich, fremdes

Blut zu verstehen: ich hasse die lesenden Mussigganger." ("It is not easily possible to comprehend strange blood—I hate the reading idlers.") Whitman himself knew how much he depended upon the reader's intuitive understanding: "The word I myself put primarily for the description of the *Leaves* . . . is the word Suggestiveness. I round out and finish little, if anything. . . . The reader will always have his or her part to do, just as much as I have had mine." And he also realized eventually that this was perhaps to put too great a burden upon the reader and was more than any author had a right to expect. He said to Traubel: "It has often occurred to me that perhaps all through the poems I assume too largely the responding sympathetic gifts of the reader."

Whitman often enough showed himself to be interested in the question of his acceptance at the hands of professors of literature as well as by the people. He said to Traubel: "I need toning down or up or something to get me in presentable form for the ceremonials of the seats of learning." And again: *"Leaves of Grass* might get benefit of clergy—benefit of professors, critics—by a liberal construction of the traditions: but I suppose it would have to be damned liberal." He was skeptical about the possibility of academic acceptance because, as he put it: "The university is only contemporary at the best: it is never prophetic: it goes, but not in advance: often indeed . . . has its eyes set in the back of its head."

It was the hopelessness of being faced with this situation that some-times resulted in the bitter and resentful disillusion which overtook him—moods which find no place in the conventional picture of the eternally optimistic, buoyant (even blustery) Whitman that is usually presented for our inspection: "No doubt the literary, professional fellows may take hold of us if we last, but I confess I shrink from it with horror. . . . The great function of the critic is to say bright things—sparkle, effervesce: probably three-quarters, perhaps even more, of them do not take the trouble to examine what they start out to criticize—to judge a man from his own standpoint, to even find out what that standpoint is."

The reaction extended occasionally as far as his own professed dis-ciples, as he told Traubel: "I get humors—they come over me—when I resent being discussed at all, whether for good or bad—almost resent the good more than the bad: such emotional revolts: against you all, against myself: against words—God damn them, words—even the words I myself utter: wondering if anything was ever done worthwhile except in the final silences." On the other hand, there were moods in which he was insatiable for attention, of whatever kind it might be, when he could have said with Oscar Wilde that the only thing worse than being talked about was not being talked about. Traubel spoke to him of some unfavorable criticism. Whitman replied: "It was not favorable? What does that matter? I like to see, to hear, all that is said provided it is serious—presents a point of view: I don't care what side it looks at me from so it looks honestly."

Again he said: "No one could have more doubts of me than I have of myself. I'm not sure of anything except my intentions." And yet underneath all the appearances of ambivalence and ambiguity, it strikes me that he was a deeply integrated character who was as sincere as any man ever was when he said: "I care nothing at all for some of the brazen art: the mere exhibitions of skillful painting: they rather horrify than attract me—are something like treason. I think of art as something to serve the people—the mass: when it fails to do that it's false to its promises: just as if a man would issue a note which from the first he has no intention of paying."

And in the same vein: "Anything which tends to keep art, books, writing, poetry, pictures, music, on the level where the people are, without untoward decoration, without haughty academic reserves, has your assent as well as mine."

He was, in addition to being a man of integrity, a man of sanity and moral balance beyond the reach or understanding of his self-styled philosophical and rationalist detractors. Who but a spiritually healthy person could have hewed out these paradoxes (which go down so deep into the heart of things) not in careful writing but extempore in speech? "We must be resigned, but not too much so: we must be calm but not too calm: we must not give in—yet we must give in some: that is, we must grade our rebellion and conformity both." Whitman could have taken for his motto the couplet of Blake's:

> Do what you will, this world's a fiction
> And made up of contradiction.

Having found a stance for himself in the midst of all the conflicts by which he was torn, he was in possession, in the latter part of his life, of a great calm and what might be called a creatively conservative temperament. That he should have passed for so long (and in some quarters even now) as a dangerous and unsettling radical is, as Richard Chase and Leslie Fiedler both remind us in this book, an almost classic case of critical misinterpretation. To the quotation which Chase cites:

"Be radical, be radical, be not too damned radical," might be added the even more emphatic expression to Traubel: "I am not afraid of conservatism, not afraid of going too slow, of being held back: rather I often wonder if we are not going ahead too swiftly—whether it's not good to have the radicalities, progresses, reforms, restrained. The fact remains that we must hold our horses, that we must not rush aimlessly ahead."

This general attitude is borne out by his attitude to specific historical characters. Lincoln, upon whom he lavished some of his finest poetry, was the example of political as well as personal conduct and "Lincoln . . . pursued a conservative policy. Lincoln, the sublime, patient Lincoln." On the other hand, he was never inclined favorably to the character of John Brown, who from the beginning became the martyr-hero of all "the radicalities" and even of some of those, like Emerson, who could not have been so described. More than thirty years after Brown's death, Whitman said to Traubel: "I, for my part, could never see in John Brown himself, merely of himself, the evidence of great human quality."

Possibly the most dramatic illustration of his growing conservatism with his maturer years is contained in his change of attitude toward the classics. In the Preface to the 1855 edition of *Leaves*, in the interest of encouraging the growth of a native American literature, he had been almost contemptuous of what the past had bequeathed to this country. Certainly a haughty condescension breathes out of his words there: "As if it were necessary to trot back generation after generation to the eastern records!" But by the time he wrote *Democratic Vistas* in 1871, his attitude toward the past and these same "eastern records" which represented the past had become so reverent that he was ready to forgo all the material wealth of the United States rather than risk losing any of them: "All the best experience of humanity, folded, saved, freighted to us here. Some of these tiny ships we call Old and New Testament, Homer, Aeschylus, Plato, Juvenal, etc. Precious minims! I think, if we were forced to choose, rather than have you, and the likes of you, and what belongs to and has grown out of you, blotted out and gone, we could better afford, appalling as that would be, to lose all actual ships, this day fastened by wharf, or floating on wave, and see them, with all their cargoes, scuttled and sent to the bottom."

It would be wrong to say that Whitman was ever converted to the doctrine of original sin, yet he came close in his later years to a recognition of the existence of evil in the world—a recognition which has often been denied to him. There is a serious overtone, in spite of the joking manner, I think, in his remark to Traubel: "Oh, the human being is a bad critter: as the old Emperor Frederick would say, we're a bad lot—a bad lot, taken all in all." Well may he have believed it, for he had known in his life misfortune and disillusion, including perhaps the bitterest of all—the lack of faith in some of those who are the closest to us through birth or circumstance. Whitman told Traubel: "My brother George once said to me: 'Walt, hasn't the world made it plain that it'd rather not have your book? Why, then, don't you call the game off?' I couldn't give George any reason he would have understood. . . . I said nothing."

But in spite of all his experience, Whitman's good spirits were sustained to the end by his few faithful friends, by his feeling for the future, and by his memory of Emerson. Though the sweetness of Emerson's memory had been somewhat spoiled for him by reported remarks over the years which revealed only too clearly the "bad critter" that struggled for mastery in the breast of "the sage of Concord" as in that of every other man, nevertheless the helping hand he had offered Whitman at the beginning and in the vital junctures remained an all-important consolation. He had done so both in writing and in speech. Whitman as an old man recalled that Emerson had said to him: "The world will come your way in the end because you have put it in your debt and such obligations are always acknowledged and met."

And it might be said that finally, with such occasional falterings as flesh is heir to, Whitman, if we credit his words to Traubel, believed as much: "I think I can say without egotism: I am destined to have an audience: There is very little sign of it now—my friends are only a few at best scattered here and there across the globe: that does not disprove me, does not make me doubtful: I still see the audience beyond: maybe in the tomorrow or the tomorrow of tomorrow."

III

If I regret any omission from the points of view which our essayists in this book have taken of Whitman it is that none of them has attempted to come to grips with him as a precursor of an intensity of American national feeling, which has never yet reached its climax. His controversial catalogues, especially of geographical place names, are nothing but the roll call of the nation, and I have felt in myself the responsive thrill of pride when memories of my own were touched upon in his verse (somehow the river of my native city seems enhanced by his calling it "beautiful, masculine Hudson") which men of earlier cultures must surely have known upon finding themselves and their associations incorporated in the national poems. The very qualities of Whitman which once made me suspicious of his motivations in the days when Hitler and Mussolini gave a bad name to every legitimate national aspiration have become increasingly the most important in my mind.

More and more I am trying to grasp his work from his own point of view and according to his own intentions. The last words of his *A Backward Glance o'er Travel'd Roads* had been written on the importance of the national theme:

"I say no land or people or circumstances ever existed so needing a race of singers and poems differing from all others, and rigidly their own, as the land and people and circumstances of our United States need such singers and poems today, and for the future. Still further, as long as the States continue to absorb and be dominated by the poetry of the Old World, and remain unsupplied with autochthonous song, to express, vitalize and give color to and define their material and political success, and minister to them distinctively, so long will they stop short of first-class Nationality and remain defective. . . .

"Concluding with two items for the imaginative genius of the West, when it worthily rises—First, what Herder taught to the young Goethe, that really great poetry is always (like the Homeric or Biblical canticles) the result of a national spirit, and not the privilege of a polish'd and select few; Second, that the strongest and sweetest songs yet remain to be sung."

The close of the passage is especially suggestive. Whitman is nothing if not the precursor of things to come. And in saying this I do not mean more Carl Sandburgs, Thomas Wolfes, or Hart Cranes (noteworthy as some of their tries to fulfill his hopes for a national song are), but Virgil! When the true classic comes to justify him, it may be possible for some critic of the future to say of Whitman what Quintilian once said of Ennius: "Let us revere him as we revere the sacred groves, hallowed by antiquity, whose massive and venerable oak trees are not so remarkable for beauty as for the religious awe which they inspire."

Until the final pattern becomes clear to all and the self-confident sterilities of this cynical age are overcome, each defender of Whitman must resign himself to being a part of the garrison of a besieged stronghold with dwindling resources and no visible sign of relief. He will need something that Napoleon referred to as "three o'clock in the morning courage." Those alone will remain steadfast to the end who feel as Whitman did that the future belongs to them and who have that rocklike reassurance from which alone can spring the invincible accents heard in every syllable of the lines from *Song of Myself*:

> My foothold is tenon'd and mortis'd in granite,
> I laugh at what you call dissolution,
> And I know the amplitude of time.

As this book is being prepared for the press, an article in *The* (London) *Times Literary Supplement* (September 17, 1954) entitled "The Living American Classics" invites my attention because it is based on assumptions so contrary to my own. Of our subject, it has this to say: "Whitman protested his Americanism so often and so violently that the protest convinces, becomes a principal theme of the poems for many readers, and so reduces the true value of the poetry. Nationalistic self-consciousness is but a petty trait in a poet; Whitman was far greater, far more concerned with the universal than his pretence would allow. *Leaves of Grass* is a classic, not because Whitman saw himself as the arch-priest of Americanism, nor yet because he imagined that Americanism was the apotheosis of man's achievement, but because, in his wisdom, he could but realize by what awful lapses America had fallen from its ideals—and if America, then also the rest of the civilized world . . ."

These statements are at the same time so ordinary and so wrong that it is not easy even to begin the analysis which I wish to make of them. For a critic of this temper, as for many of the teachers of literature in our colleges today, the apex of Whitman's achievement is represented by *Democratic Vistas*, and the *Vistas* in such hands become an unrelieved negation of everything that Whitman is supposed to stand for. Whitman, in a perverse interpretation, is transformed into his own opposite, becomes the great denier and skeptic of the values of the American culture which he everywhere so strenuously defends.

That *Democratic Vistas* was born of a soul-shaking reappraisal of some kind in Whitman is evident enough to the sensitive reader, but that it becomes in any sense a backsliding into a morass of poisonous doubt out of which the poet saw it as his function from the beginning to raise his fainthearted countrymen is an interpretation that must not be allowed. It is my own feeling that *Democratic Vistas*, in terms of an analogy supplied by the religious life, represents "the dark night of the soul," which Whitman, like other believers in history, had to traverse during the greatest crisis of his life. Had he never emerged from his despair into an area of serenity, we would have heard nothing more of him. The emergence is evident not only after the writing of *Demo-*

cratic Vistas but within the *Vistas* themselves. Those who are discouraged with the possibilities of America seem to take a vicarious delight in the struggle of Whitman with his demon, just as if he had been overcome in the struggle and not victorious. It may be argued that my way of stating the matter is too blatant, perhaps out of an excess of polemical zeal, and that some of the very things I myself have said earlier (as well as those to be said later in the book by some of the essayists) may be used to justify a reinterpretation of Whitman as something other than a Professional American or a simple-minded Booster, but the correction of this misconception must not be the excuse for a distortion in another direction even more pernicious in its consequences.

"Nationalistic self-consciousness is but a petty trait in a poet [which] reduces the true value of the poetry." This assertion (catering as it does to a fashionable contemporary prejudice among intellectuals and deriving a specious plausibility from this prejudice) is effectively refuted by the simple question: "Why?" Neither logic nor experience seems to be on the side of the critic. Without pausing to cavil at the uncertainties in the meaning of the key terms of his statement ("nationalistic," "self-consciousness"), it may be remarked that three of the greatest artistic figures of the nineteenth century (to go back no further) were all intensely partisan in favor of the national groups into which they had been born—Wagner, Dostoevski, and Whitman himself. The first was Pan-German, the second Pan-Slavic, and the last Pan-American long before that term was coined and with a far more dynamic meaning attached to it than was afterward to be the case. Each of these great men foresaw his own nation in a messianic role to redeem humanity and was powerfully inspired by his vision. It is easy to speak of "the universal" and to contrast it with "nationalistic self-consciousness," but, like the poet's fancy, love of humanity as a whole, to achieve form and meaning, has to be tied down to "a local habitation and a name." Is it not instructive to reflect on the apparent paradox that those who have achieved the most widespread recognition from the world have been the ones who began by being circumscribed in their loyalties and attachments? Man realizes man*kind* by feeling for his own kin, and those who wish to skip that initial step in their quest for the ultimate, or neglect the specific and concrete embodiment in favor of an abstract formula, often end by being equally unfaithful to all sides. For it may be asked in the language of the Scriptures, what shall it profit a man to imagine that he loves the whole world when he has lost all sense of personal identification, which is always a matter first of parochial connections. Dostoevski is so deeply Russian that he speaks convincingly to all men; Wagner is so German and Whitman so American that they speak to the feelings of all men regardless of boundaries. The road to the universal leads *through* the particular and not away from the particular. The only writers of a universal language who have thus far appeared are those who have written their own language well enough to interest men of an alien tongue in learning it. Not the Esperantists or the exponents of Basic English but Plato has come closest to the ideal of creating a language intelligible to all men.

When we speak of Whitman the thought of Lincoln is never very far away. In the Gettysburg Address, so much has been made of the phrases about "government of the people," etc., that not too much notice is taken of the fact that Lincoln begins by speaking of the emergence of America as "a new nation." We may say that the active realization of all the implications latent in this expression is still, after a century, very far from being complete. Whitman presents us with a similar challenge. In the Preface of '55, after saying that "The United States themselves are essentially the greatest poem" (he must mean, at any rate, the greatest one that has not yet been composed), Whitman goes on to define the States as "not merely a nation but a teeming nation of nations." That expression seems to me to contain the ideal against which we ought to measure all our accomplishments; it is very much more satisfactory and sensitive a description of what we are trying to become than that "melting-pot" theory which bears a superficial resemblance to it.

Whitman and not his critic seems right in assuming that his national idealism, far from being a petty trait of his work, is the informing agent of all that is most durable in him. It is this quality precisely that, far from having exhausted its potentialities in the first century of his survival, has not yet begun the really important work for which it seems destined. To paraphrase a well-known saying of Whitman's about the mutual dependence of poets and audiences, it may be justly said that to have great nations, you must have great poets also. Though ancient Rome in actuality may never have lived up to Virgil's dream of her in the *Aeneid*, though England may never have been quite worthy of the words devoted to her glory by Shakespeare or Milton, though Russia shows no signs of fulfilling the generous aspirations of Dostoevski, and though modern Germany has made a travesty of Wagner's dramas while attempting to imitate them, yet it remains a fact that the educators of the best examples of each national type remain the poets. America at the moment may not be close to Whitman's far-

seeing vision (though perhaps not as far as it seems to some people—
for he predicted a future in which we, "Liberty's nation . . . completely arm'd and victorious, and very haughty," would confront the
rest of the world "with Law on one side and Peace on the other"—
suggesting a sternness of martial demeanor almost primitively Moham-
medan in character) ; but even if it were to be admitted that we are at
an infinite distance from the image of us which he saw in his mind's
eye, what does that really matter? It cannot be said that there is no
relation at all between his image and the reality of America, or that
Whitman willfully deranged his senses like Rimbaud and insisted upon
seeing romantic mosques in place of the prosaic, brick factories which
surrounded him! Are we at the end of our history as a nation or but
very little advanced from the beginning? Should we succumb to that
despair which he himself overcame in *Democratic Vistas*? Or be
goaded by him into ever greater efforts to make ourselves worthy of
his affection? To the end that we all may, both individually and col-
lectively as a nation (as "simple, separate persons" and "en masse"),
dare to regard ourselves as we really are, without flinching, in that
mirror of heroic proportions which he erected for our future on this
continent and which can never be taken down again. The poet's Father-
land is always constructed in the image of his heart's desire ; does this
fact invalidate it as a criterion for the judgment of reality? If we are
not the last hope of earth, we must try to be the best hope of earth according to the instruction of our noblest minds. It seems to me that
every generation that would truly live owes no less than that effort to
itself.

An Essay on *Leaves of Grass*

LEAVES OF GRASS! It was a good title for a book of poems, especially for a new book of American poems. It was a challenge to the entire concept of the poetic idea, and from a new viewpoint, a rebel viewpoint, an American viewpoint. In a word and at the beginning it enunciated a shocking truth, that the common ground is of itself a poetic source. There had been inklings before this that such was the case in the works of Robert Burns and the poet Wordsworth, but in this instance the very forms of the writing had been altered: it had gone over to the style of the words as they appeared on the page. Whitman's so-called "free verse" was an assault on the very citadel of the poem itself; it constituted a direct challenge to all living poets to show cause why they should not do likewise. It is a challenge that still holds good after a century of vigorous life during which it has been practically continuously under fire but never defeated.

From the beginning Whitman realized that the matter was largely technical. It had to be free verse or nothing with him and he seldom varied from that practice—and never for more than the writing of an occasional poem. It was a sharp break, and if he was to go astray he had no one but himself to blame for it. It was a technical matter, true enough, and he would stick it out to the end, but to do any more with it than simply to write the poems was beyond him.

He had seen a great light but forgot almost at once after the first revelation everything but his "message," the idea which originally set him in motion, the idea on which he had been nurtured, the idea of democracy—and took his eye off the words themselves which should have held him.

The point is purely academic—the man had his hands full with the conduct of his life and couldn't, if they had come up, be bothered with other matters. As a result, he made no further progress as an artist but, in spite of various topical achievements, continued to write with diminishing effectiveness for the remainder of his life.

He didn't know any better. He didn't have the training to construct his verses after a conscious mold which would have given him power over them to turn them this way, then that, at will. He only knew how to give them birth and to release them to go their own way. He was preoccupied with the great ideas of the time, to which he was devoted, but, after all, poems are made out of words not ideas. He never showed any evidence of knowing this and the unresolved forms consequent upon his beginnings remained in the end just as he left them.

Verses, in English, are frequently spoken of as measures. It is a fortunate designation as it gives us, in looking at them, the idea of elapsed time. We are reminded that the origin of our verse was the dance—and even if it had not been the dance, the heart when it is stirred has its multiple beats, and verse at its most impassioned sets the heart violently beating. But as the heart picks up we also begin to count. Finally, the measure for each language and environment is accepted. In English it is predominantly the iambic pentameter, but whether that is so for the language Whitman spoke is something else again. It is a point worth considering, but apart from the briefest of notices a point not to be considered here. It may be that the essential pace of the English and the American languages is diametrically opposed each to the other and that that is an important factor in the writing of their poetry, but that is for the coming generations to discover. Certainly not only the words but the meter, the measure that governed Whitman's verses, was not English. But there were more pressing things than abstract discussions of meter to be dealt with at that time and the poet soon found himself involved in them.

Very likely the talk and the passionate talk about freedom had affected him as it had infected the French and many others earlier. It is said that, when as a young man he lived in New Orleans, he had fallen in love with a beautiful octoroon but had allowed his friends and relatives to break up the match. It is possible that the disappointment determined the pattern of his later rebellion in verse. Free verse was his great idea! *Versos sueltos* the Spanish call them. It is not an entirely new idea, but it was entirely new to the New York Yankee who was, so to speak, waiting for it with open arms and an overcharged soul and the example of Thomas Jefferson to drive him on.

But verse had always been, for Englishmen and the colonials that imitated them, a disciplined maneuver of the intelligence, as it is today, in which measure was predominant. They resented this American with his new idea, and attacked him in a characteristic way — *on moral grounds*. And he fell for it. He had no recourse but to defend himself and the fat was in the fire. How could verse be free without being immoral? There is something to it. It is the same attack, with a more modern tilt to it, that undoubtedly bothers T. S. Eliot. He is one of the best informed of our writers and would do us a great service, if free verse—mold it as he will—is not his choice, to find us an alternative. From the evidence, he has tried to come up with just that, but up to the present writing he has not brought the thing off.

The case of Mr. Eliot is in this respect interesting. He began writing at Harvard from a thoroughly well-schooled background and produced a body of verse that was immediately so successful that when his poem *The Waste Land* was published, it drove practically everyone else from the field. Ezra Pound, who had helped him arrange the poem on the page, was confessedly jealous. Other American poets had to take second place. A new era, under domination of a return to a study of the classics, was gratefully acknowledged by the universities, and Mr. Eliot, not Mr. Pound, was ultimately given the Nobel Prize. The drift was plainly away from all that was native to America, Whitman among the rest, and toward the study of the past and England.

Though no one realized it, a violent revolution had taken place in American scholarship and the interests from which it stemmed. Eliot had completely lost interest in all things American, in the very ideology of all that America stood for, including the idea of freedom itself in any of its phases. Whitman as a symbol of indiscriminate freedom was completely antipathetic to Mr. Eliot, who now won the country away from him again. The tendency toward freedom in the verse forms, which seemed to be thriving among American poets, was definitely checked and the stage was taken over for other things. I shall never forget the impression created by *The Waste Land*; it was as if the bottom had dropped out of everything. I had not known how much the spirit of Whitman animated us until it was withdrawn from us. Free verse became overnight a thing of the past. Men went about congratulating themselves as upon the disappearance of something that had disturbed their dreams; and indeed it was so—the dreams of right-thinking students of English verse had long been disturbed by the appearance among them of the horrid specter of Whitman's free verse. Now it was as if a liberator, a Saint George, had come just in the nick of time to save them. The instructors in all the secondary schools were grateful.

Meanwhile, Mr. Eliot had become a British subject and removed himself to England where he took up residence. He became a member of the Church of England. He was determined to make the break with America complete, as his fellow artist Henry James had done before him, and began to publish such poems as *Ash Wednesday* and the play *Murder in the Cathedral*, and the *Four Quartets*. Something had happened to him, something drastic, something to do, doubtless, with man's duty and his freedom in the world. It is a far cry from this to Whitman's thought of man as a free agent. The pendulum had gone the full swing.

It is inevitable for us to connect the happenings in the world generally with what takes place in the poem. When Mr. Eliot quit writing, when he quit writing poems, it looked as if he had got to a point where he had nowhere else to turn, and as if in his despair he had given up not only the poem but the world. A man as clever and well informed as he was had the whole world at his feet, but the only conclusion that he reached was that he wanted none of it. Especially did he want none of the newer freedom.

Not that he didn't in his verse try it on, for size, let us say, in his later experiments, particularly in *Four Quartets*, but even there he soon came to the end of his rope. The accented strophe he had definitely given up, as Wagner in the prelude to *Parsifal* had done the same, but to infer from that fact that he had discovered the freedom of a new measure was not true. It looked to me, at least, as if there were some profound depth to his probing beyond which he dared not go without compromising his religious faith. He did not attempt it. It is useful to record the limits of his penetration and the point at which he gave up his attempts to penetrate further. Just how far shall we go in our search for freedom and, more importantly, how shall our efforts toward a greater freedom be conditioned in our verses? All these decisions, which must be reached in deciding what to do, have implications of general value in our lives.

The young men who are students of literature today in our universities do not believe in seeking within the literary forms, the lines, the foot, the way in which to expand their efforts to know the universe, as Whitman did, but are content to follow the theologians and Mr. Eliot. In that, they are children of the times; they risk nothing, for by risking an expanded freedom you are very likely to come a cropper. What, in the words of Hjalmar Ekdahl in *The Wild Duck,* are you going to invent?

Men, offering their heads, have always come up with new proposals, and the world of events waits upon them, and who shall say whether it were better to close one's eyes or go forward like Galileo to the light or wait content in the darkness like the man in the next county? Whitman went forward to what to him seemed desirable, and so if we are to reject him entirely we must at least follow him at the start to find out what his discoveries were intended to signify and what not to signify.

Certainly, we are in our day through with such loose freedom as he employed in his verses in the blind belief that it was all going to come out right in the end. We know now that it is not. But are we, because of that, to give up freedom entirely? Merely to put down the lines as they happen to come into your head will not make a poem, and if, as happened more than once in Whitman's case, a poem result, who is going to tell what he has made? The man knew what he was doing, but he did not know all he was doing. Much still remains to discover, but that freedom in the conduct of the verses is desirable cannot be questioned.

There is a very moving picture of Whitman facing the breakers coming in on the New Jersey shore, when he heard the onomatopoeic waves talk to him direct in a Shakespearean language which might have been Lear himself talking to the storm. But it was not what it seemed; it was a new language, an unnamed language which Whitman could not identify or control.

For as the English had foreseen, this freedom of which there had been so much talk had to have limits somewhere. If not, it would lead you astray. That was the problem. And there was at about that time a whole generation of Englishmen, prominent among whom was Frank Harris, whom it did lead astray in moral grounds, just as there were Frenchmen at the time of the French Revolution who were led astray and are still being led astray under the difficult conditions that exist today. It is the reaction against such patterns of thought that moved Eliot and that part of the present generation which is not swallowed up by its fascination with the scene which draws them to Paris whenever they get the opportunity to go there. For in your search for freedom—which is desirable—you must stop somewhere, but where exactly shall you stop? Whitman could not say.

To propose that the answer to the problem should lie in the verse itself would have been to those times an impertinence—and the same would be the case even now. The Greeks had their Dionysia in the spring of the year, when morals could be forgotten, and then the control of life resumed its normal course. In other words, they departmentalized their lives, being of an orderly cast of mind, but we do not lend ourselves easily to such a solution. With us it is all or nothing, provided we are not caught at it. Either we give ourselves to a course of action or we do not give ourselves. Either we are to be free men or not free men—at least in theory. Whitman, like Tom Paine, recognized no limits and that got him into trouble.

But the waves on the Jersey shore still came tumbling in, quieting him as their secret escaped him, isolating him and leaving him lonesome—but possessed by the great mystery which won the world to his side. For he was unquestionably the child of the years. What was the wave that moved the dawning century also moved him and demanded his recognition, and it was not to be denied. All the discoveries and inventions which were to make the twentieth century exceed all others, for better or worse, were implicit in his work. He surpassed the ritualistic centuries which preceded him, just as Ehrlich and Koch and finally Einstein were to exceed Goethe. It was destined to be so, and the New World of which he was a part gave him birth. He had invented a new way of assaulting fate. "Make new!" was to him as it was to Pound much later on an imperious command which completely controlled him.

If he was to enlarge his opportunity he needed room, in verse as in everything else. But there were to be no fundamental changes in the concepts that keep our lives going at an accepted pace and within normal limits. The line was still to be the line, quite in accord with the normal contours of our accepted verse forms. It is not so much that which brought Whitman's verse into question but the freedom with which he laid it on the page. There he had abandoned all sequence and all order. It was as if a tornado had struck.

A new order had hit the world, a relative order, a new measure with which no one was familiar. The thing that no one realized, and this includes Whitman himself, is that the native which they were dealing with was no longer English but a new language akin to the New World to which its nature accorded in subtle ways that they did not recognize. That made all the difference. And not only was it new to America—it was new to the world. There was to be a new measure applied to all things, for there was to be a new order operative in the world. But it has to be insisted on that it was not disorder. Whitman's verses seemed disorderly, but ran according to an unfamiliar and a difficult measure. It was an order which was essential to the new world, not only of the poem, but to the world of chemistry and physics. In this way, the man was more of a prophet than he knew. The full significance of his innovations in the verse patterns has not yet been fully disclosed.

The change in the entire aesthetic of American art as it began to differ not only from British but from all the art of the world up to this time was due to this tremendous change in measure, a relative measure, which he was the first to feel and to embody in his works. What he was leaving behind did not seem to oppress him, but it oppressed the others and rightly so.

It is time now to look at English and American verse at the time Whitman began to write, for only by so doing can we be led to discover what he did and the course that lay before him. He had many formidable rivals to face on his way to success. But his chief opponent was, as he well knew, the great and medieval Shakespeare. And if any confirmation of Shakespeare's sacrosanct position in the language is still sought it is easily to be obtained when anything is breathed mentioning some alteration in the verse forms which he distinguished by using them. He may be imitated as Christopher Fry imitates him, but to vary or depart from him is heresy. Taken from this viewpoint, the clinical sheets of Shakespeare as a writer are never much studied. That he was the greatest word-man that ever existed in the language or out of it is taken for granted but there the inquiry ends.

Shakespeare presented Whitman with a nut hard to crack. What to do with the English language? It was all the more of a problem since the elements of it could not be presented at all or even recognized to exist. As far as the English language was concerned, there was only to use it and to use it well according to the great tradition of the masters.

And indeed it was a magnificent tradition. At the beginning of the seventeenth century it had reached an apogee which it had, to a great extent, maintained to the present day and of which it was proud and jealous. But when Shakespeare wrote, the laurels were new and had so recently been attained and had come from such distinguished achievements that the world seemed to pause for breath. It was a sort of noon and called for a halt. The man himself seemed to feel it and during an entire lifetime did no more than develop to the full his talents. It was noon sure enough for him, and he had only to stretch out in the sun and expand his mood.

Unlike Whitman, he was or represented the culmination of a historic as well as literary past whose forms were just coming to a head after the great trials which were to leave their marks on the centuries. There had been Chaucer, but the language had come of age since then as had the country. Now America had been discovered and the world could not grow much larger. Further expansion, except in a limited degree, was unlikely, so that the poet was left free to develop his world of detail but was not called upon to extend it. More was not necessary than to find something to do and develop it for the entire span of a long life. But as always with the artist, selection was an important point in the development.

For instance, as his sonnets show, Shakespeare was an accomplished rhymer, but he gave it up early. The patches of heroic couplet which he wrote for the Players in *Hamlet* are among the best examples of that form. Yet his main reliance was on blank verse—though he did, on occasion, try his hand at a triple accent which he rejected without more than a thought. The demands of the age called for other things and he was, above everything else, a practical man.

Practicing for so long a time upon the iambic pentameter, he had the opportunity to develop himself prodigiously in it. Over the years he shows a technical advance, a certain impatience with restraint in his work which makes it loose and verges more toward the conformation of prose. There is a great difference between Shakespeare's earlier and later work, the latter being freer and more natural in tone.

A feeling for prose began to be felt all through his verse. But at his death the form began to lapse rapidly into the old restrictions. It got worse and worse with the years until all the Elizabethan tenor had been stripped away, or as Milton phrased it speaking of his illustrious predecessor :

> Sweetest Shakespeare, Nature's child,
> Warbled his native woodnotes wild.

With Milton came Cromwell and the English Revolution, and Shakespeare was forgotten, together with the secrets of his versification, just as Whitman today is likely to be forgotten and the example of his verses and all that refers to him.

The interest that drove Whitman on is the same one that drove Shakespeare at the end of his life in an attempt to enlarge the scope of written verse, to find more of expression in the forms of the language employed. But the consequences of such experimentation are always drastic and amount in the end to its suppression, which in the person of a supreme genius is not easy.

From what has been said thus far, you can see why it is impossible to imitate Shakespeare ; he was part of a historic process which cannot repeat itself. All imitations of the forms of the past are meaningless, empty shells, which have merely the value of decorations. So that, if anything is now to be created, it must be in a new form. Whitman, if he was to do anything of moment, could not, no matter how much he may have bowed down to the master, imitate him. It would not have had any meaning at all. And his responsibility to the new language was such that he had no alternative but to do as it bade him.

Though he may not have known it, with Whitman the whole spirit of the age itself had been brought under attack. It was a blind stab which he could not identify any more than a child. How could he, no matter how acute his instincts were, have foreseen the discoveries in chemistry, in physics, in abnormal psychology, or even the invention of the telephone or the disclosure of our subterranean wealth in petroleum? He knew only, as did those who were disturbed by his free verse, that something had occurred to the normal structure of conventional aesthetic and that he could not accept it any longer. Therefore, he acted.

We have to acknowledge at once in seeking a meaning involving the complex concerns of the world that the philosophic, the aesthetic, and the mechanical are likely to stem in their development from the same root. One may be much in advance of the other in its discoveries, but in the end a great equalizing process is involved so that the discovery of the advance in the structure of the poetic line is equated by an advance in the conception of physical facts all along the line. Man has no choice in these matters; the only question is, will he recognize the changes that are taking place in time to make the proper use of them? And when time itself is conceived of as relative, no matter how abstruse that may sound, the constructions, the right constructions, cannot be accepted with a similar interpretation. It may take time to bring this about, but when a basic change has occurred in our underlying concern it brooks no interference in the way it will work itself out.

Whitman didn't know anything about this, nor does Mr. Eliot take it into his considerations nor Father Merton either, but if they had to construct a satisfactory poetic line it had and still has to be done according to this precept. For we have learned, if we have learned anything from the past, that the principles of physics are immutable. Best, if you do not approve of what writing has become, to follow in Mr. Eliot's footsteps.

For it is important to man's fate that these matters be—if anything is important to man's fate in this modern world. At least, you cannot retrace steps that have been taken in the past. And you don't know, you simply do not know, what may come of it. No more than Whitman knew what his struggle to free verse may have implied and may still imply for us no matter how, at the moment, the world may have forsaken him. The books are not closed even though the drift in the tide of our interest may at the moment be all the other way. It cannot so soon have reversed itself. Something is still pending, though the final shape of the thing has not yet crystallized. Perhaps that is the reason for the regression. There are too many profitable leads in other associated fields of the intelligence for us to draw back now.

Where have the leads which are *not* aesthetic tended to take us in the present century? By paying attention to detail and our telescopes and microscopes and the reinterpretations of their findings, we realize that man has long since broken from the confinement of the more rigid of his taboos. It is reasonable to suppose that he will in the future, in spite of certain setbacks, continue to follow the same course.

Man finds himself on the earth whether he likes it or not, with nowhere else to go. What then is to become of him? Obviously we can't stand still or we shall be destroyed. Then if there is no room for us on the outside we shall, in spite of ourselves, have to go *in*: into the cell, the atom, the poetic line, for our discoveries. We have to break the old apart to make room for ourselves, whatever may be our tragedy and however we may fear it. By making room within the line itself for his inventions, Whitman revealed himself to be a worthy and courageous man of his age and, to boot, a farseeing one.

Go-Befores and Embryons

A Biographical Reprise

CONSIDER the unknown poet who in the spring of 1855 was revising and editing his first volume of poems. He set the type himself at the printing establishment of Andrew and James Rome in Brooklyn. When the volume was published in July, its readers beheld a thin, dark-green quarto containing twelve poems and bearing, on the cover, the ornate curves of gilded lettering which announced, with the help of symbolic grasses and flowers, that the title of the book was *Leaves of Grass*. Although the author did not declare his name in the usual manner, a certain "Walt Whitman" was referred to, in one of the poems, as "an American, one of the roughs, a Kosmos." Interested readers, of whom there were few, might have discovered that the copyright was held by "Walter Whitman." And no reader could miss the portrait, which served as frontispiece, of a bearded man of somewhat indeterminate age, dressed in shirt sleeves and broad-brimmed hat, his dark undershirt visible at the neck, his body carelessly at ease, his extraordinary, heavy-lidded eyes enigmatic in their indolent introspection. If this man was a kosmos and one of the roughs, he was, it appeared, a somewhat relaxed kosmos and a gentle, distinctly faunlike rough. Whitman printed about a thousand copies of his book and sold almost none.

Except for a mixed batch of reviews, the response was limited to a few of the literary men—notably Emerson—to whom the author hopefully sent his volume. It would be a long time before the world was ready to admit that one of the remarkable books of the nineteenth century had issued from Rome Brothers printing house. But neither the book of poems nor the extraordinary man pictured on the frontispiece had leapt out of the void. They had developed slowly and uncertainly, more so than most poems and poets. In his letter of congratulation to Whitman, Emerson expressed some inferential curiosity about the "long foreground" which he knew must precede *Leaves of Grass*. It is not our purpose here to present a detailed view of this long foreground but merely to mention some of its representative episodes.

Whitman was born into a declining family which tended in the poet's generation to run out into the sands of neurosis, idiocy, poverty, sickness, and hard luck. He was the second of nine children. Of these one brother, Andrew, became a drunkard and, after imposing a slatternly and loose-principled wife on his mother's hospitality, died of tuberculosis at thirty-seven. Another brother Jesse contracted syphilis and died after years in an insane asylum. The youngest brother, Eddie, was an imbecile and epileptic. Walt's favorite sister, Hannah, though gifted, became squalid, eccentric, and unbalanced during a long and harrowing marriage to an indigent painter who tried to make an artistic career in Burlington, Vermont; she was given to spells of drunkenness and paranoia. The family life which nourished so much human failure seems to have been characterized in Walt's boyhood by a kind of moral and psychic squalor, anxiety, restlessness, and vagrancy, and there can be no doubt that Whitman's lifelong concern with cleanliness and health, which borders sometimes on the crankish and forms also a part of his prophetic program for democracy, was a response to his family life. The wishful image one remembers from Whitman's *Brooklyn Eagle* editorials of Manhattan surrounded by thousands of nude, healthy citizens bathing in the rivers is a utopian compensation for the squalor he had known. And the history of his brothers and sisters lends a certain concreteness to the word "sane" in the well-known phrase from "When Lilacs Last in the Dooryard Bloom'd," "O sane and sacred death."

Walt was born on May 31, 1819, at West Hills, Long Island, in the family farmhouse. Walter Whitman, the father, was the first of an extensive family line, which reached back into New England, to leave farming. He became a carpenter, it being his practice to build a house and then move into it until it was sold or lost to creditors. Although the Whitmans do not seem to have lived in actual hardship, they did not live so well as had the earlier generations. These had enjoyed a relatively settled life and had apparently known a good deal of prosperity until, after the Revolution, the family fortunes began gradually to decline. One may doubt that Walter Whitman filled what were later to be his son's prescriptions for ideal American manhood and paternity, invoking as these did a love of comrades, an heroic frame of body and of mind, and a poetic nature. Walter Whitman is said to have been respected as a good workman, but he was generally silent and morose, and sometimes given to outbursts of anger; a photograph makes him appear puzzled and aggrieved. One is not surprised that in Walt's poetry wherever, as in the *Sea-Drift* poems, he is concerned with the metaphysical status of the self, he tends to use paternity as an image of chaos. Apart from his poetry, Walt's attitude toward his father seems to have alternated between affection and indifference. There was at least enough sympathy between them to allow them to work together at carpentering in the early 1850's; and before the father's death in 1855, Walt took him on a final visit to the countryside and the family homestead.

Whitman got some of his lifelong ideas from his father. Walter Whitman was a convinced Democrat of the Jeffersonian and Jacksonian traditions. And he had affinities even more radical, two of his heroes being Tom Paine and Elias Hicks, the dissident Quaker. He had no religion, beyond a partiality for Quakerism.

Walt's mother gave the family whatever stability and order it had. She was a more admirable person in nearly every way than her husband, and the worship of his mother is of course one of the most striking facts about the poet's life. In *Specimen Days* Whitman recorded his impressions upon revisiting for the first time in more than forty years the scenes of his childhood (except for the trip with his father mentioned above). In these notes he exhibits that haunting sense of mystery with which he always regarded "the go-befores and embryons," the roots of things. Poking about the old homestead he is mystified and reverential. The decaying graves of his ancestors, and indeed the whole scene, he finds, as he keeps saying, "sterile." Yet, if there is anything vital among the images his memory resurrects, it is his mother's family, the Van Velsors. Of the Van Velsor homestead he writes, ". . . the whole scene, with what it arous'd, memories of my young days there half a century ago, the vast kitchen and ample fireplace and sitting room adjoining, the plain furniture, the meals, the house full of merry people, my grandmother Amy's sweet old face in its Quaker cap, my grandfather, 'the Major,' jovial, red, stout, with sonorous voice and characteristic physiognomy, with actual sights themselves, made the most pronounc'd half-day's experience of my whole jaunt." Walt Whitman gained from his mother the stubborn perseverance upon which he could count in periods of adversity, and perhaps also an inwardness and sense of mystery. These qualities were confirmed in the mother by her Quaker beliefs and in her son by that strain of Quaker feeling which is observable in him. Despite their sober virtues, however, the Van Velsors were a more various and vivid family than the Whitmans, and Walt records the fact that his "mother, as a young woman, was a daily and daring rider." Still, there was little of vividness, variety, or gaiety in the environment in which Walt himself grew up. The picture of his mother, taken in advancing years, makes her look, with her strong, broad face, somewhat resigned and sad; yet she has an air of triumph, of endurance, of humor, of worldly wisdom. Whitman's description of a family scene in "There Was a Child Went Forth" strikes one as referring authentically to his own parents:

> The mother at home quietly placing the dishes on the supper-table,
> The mother with mild words, clean her cap and gown, a wholesome odor falling off her person and clothes as she walks by,
> The father, strong, self-sufficient, manly, mean, anger'd, unjust,
> The blow, the quick loud word, the tight bargain, the crafty lure . . .

There is much evidence, such as the series of touching letters that passed between them in the Civil War period, that the attachment between Walt and his mother was both close and lifelong. The mother was almost illiterate and never understood in the least the poems her son wrote.

But despite the mother's influence one's general impression of the family life, as I have said, is of laxity and of restless anxiety. As Holloway observed, there was little sense of common purpose or family solidarity. Possibly the influence of this mode of life on the later Whitman is suggested in the lines from "There Was a Child Went Forth" which follow immediately those quoted above:

> The family usages, the language, the company, the furniture, the yearning and swelling heart,
> Affection that will not be gainsay'd, the sense of what is real, the thought if after all it should prove unreal,
> The doubts of day-time and the doubts of night-time, the curious whether and how,
> Whether that which appears so is so, or is it all flashes and specks?

On other occasions too Whitman is accustomed to embark from a reminiscence of his father and mother upon the moral and metaphysical question of what is "real" and what is "unreal." His lifelong concern with "identity" and his many speculations as to how identity can be formed or maintained or eluded may be traced to the unsettled family life of his earliest days.

In 1823 the Whitmans moved to Brooklyn, then a town of 7,000 inhabitants, where the family changed, for several years, from house to house, and Walt began an irregular course of schooling. At one of the Brooklyn public schools Walt was remembered in later years to have been "a big, good-natured lad, clumsy and slovenly in appearance, but not otherwise remarkable." And this is the first of a long series of testimonials to that incorrigible indolence which is one of the salient characteristics of Walt Whitman's temperament and which is in striking contrast to his intermittent capacity for hard work and for brilliant outbursts of energy.

Walt probably left school in 1830 and from then until 1836 was employed at various jobs in and around Brooklyn and New York. We have a glimpse of the awkward, shambling, but handsome youth working as an errand boy in a lawyer's and then a doctor's office, and then learning to set type in the offices of the *Long Island Patriot* and the *Long Island Star*. We glimpse him working in 1835 and 1836 in New York printing offices and beginning that inveterate play and opera going which became for him almost a career in itself in the years before the Civil War.

In 1836 Walt left the city and returned to rural Long Island, where he was for a year or two a schoolteacher. One does not wish to burden so ordinary an occurrence with undue significance, especially since it seems to have been largely an inability to support himself in New York that drove him back to the country. Nevertheless, this was the first of those periodic withdrawals from the more highly ordered and businesslike part of the world which are noticeable throughout Whitman's life. He seems to have made one of these strategic withdrawals in the two or three years just before 1855 in preparation for the writing of *Song of Myself* and the other poems of the first edition. He made a recuperative retirement to rural Long Island in the fall of 1855 to absorb and master the disappointment of the failure of his book; he emerged from this withdrawal with the renewed determination (as he declared in the open letter to Emerson which he included in his 1856 edition of *Leaves of Grass*) to dedicate his life to poetry.

There was certainly a powerful reactionary drive in Whitman's personality, a drive too positive to be mere indolence, though of that he had aplenty. One of the characteristic acts of his life is this turning back upon himself, followed by a new advance. It may be said that all living things, and especially all creative human beings, pass through this rhythm. But in Whitman we notice a remarkable preponderance of the reactionary impulse. He seems more often than not to have been passive, psychically slothful, and attached, in a mood of mystery and reverence, to the beginnings, the primitive conditions of his life. Beneath both the frolicsomeness and prophetic egotism of his poetic sensibility, there is in Whitman an almost Proustian receptivity and capacity for retrogressive brooding.

In his own way Whitman was conscious of the heavy recalcitrancy and inertia of his being, as is suggested by some of his remarks in later life—such as, "I am a slow arriver: I get there but I always come in last," or "I am the most conservative of conservatives," a phrase to which he gave personal and psychic meanings rather than strictly political ones.

Between 1838 and 1841 Walt was working on newspapers and teaching school. For some months he was on the staff of the *Long Island Democrat*. But his most ambitious project was a paper, the *Long Islander*, which he printed himself in Huntington. At this time (1838–39) he even bought a horse on which every week he delivered the paper through the countryside; this occasioned, as he said, many happy "jaunts." It seems also to have occasioned an early bankruptcy, doubtless one of the reverses which led him to remark in later years that "the time of my boyhood was a very restless and unhappy one; I did not know what to do." An account of Walt's habits in about 1840 comes from his landlady, Mrs. Brenton, the wife of the publisher of the *Democrat*. With obvious asperity she describes him as having been slovenly, morose, and withdrawn. He disliked the children in the family; people tripped over his feet as he lolled in a chair; and, Mrs. Brenton complained, he mused and loafed under the blossoming apple trees all afternoon instead of going to the newspaper office. Yet he cannot have been wholly indolent. Considerable prose and verse remain from this period, and by 1840 he had become active in politics, campaigning locally for Van Buren and even making a speech, in July 1841, at a mass meeting organized in New York by the Tammany Society.

In the *Democrat* Whitman published a series of sketches called *Sun-Down Papers From the Desk of a Schoolmaster*. The artificial style he affected and the sentiments he espoused may be seen in paper Number 5, in which he inculcates temperance: "Amidst the universal excitement which appears to have been created of late years, with regard to the evils created by ardent spirits, it seems to have been forgotten that there are other, and almost as injurious, kinds of intemperance." He proceeds in a tone both facetious and serious to warn of the consequences of too much tea and coffee. Another sketch consists of reflections on death and remarks that when the "Pale Mower" slays an old or middle-aged person, one's grief is "coarse" and has few "refined associations." But what poetic sentiments may not be generated "when we see an infant laid away to a quiet slumber in the bosom of the great mother of men"? In other sketches he resolves to write a great book on the moral dangers of wealth; contrives an elaborate allegory demonstrating that Truth is to be seen only by the naïve; celebrates the "philosophick quietude" induced by loafing; idealizes a kind of tender and healthy but diffuse and disembodied love as against "the puerile, moping love, painted by such trashy writers as Byron and Bulwer." The *Sun-Down Papers* faithfully reflect the popular culture of the time. And, even though they were written as journeywork, they faithfully reflect, also, certain enduring qualities in the author—his abstemiousness, for example, and his preoccupation with death, his plain democratic dislike of wealth, his desire to loaf and invite his soul, his inclination toward a diffuse and nonsexual love.

There was a good deal of dull romanticism in the Whitman of these years of withdrawal. Yet beneath the surface of the pining, restless, and unhappy young man new energies were noticeably stirring. In 1841 he went back to New York and was soon embarked upon a period of relatively busy editing, writing, and politicking. And what is most striking of all, the indolent overgrown youth who lolled in his chair or under the apple trees became a dandy with a frock coat, a high hat, a cane, a flower in his lapel, and a carefully nurtured and trimmed beard. A fellow editor on the *Daily Aurora* later recalled that at twenty-two Walt looked twenty-five, was tall, graceful, and neat, and presented "a very pleasing and impressive eye and a cheerful, happy-looking countenance." Despite the brisk appearance, however, Whitman seems actually to have been, even in this relatively energtic period, a somewhat desultory editor. He is said to have made it his custom to reach the *Aurora* office late in the morning, scan the daily papers, and then stroll down Broadway to the Battery, "spending an hour or two amid the trees and enjoying the water view, returning to the office . . . at about 2 or 3 o'clock." Whitman briefly held jobs on several journals in New York and contributed to several others, among them the *Democratic Review,* whose contributors included Hawthorne, Bryant, Thoreau, Whittier, and Poe.

Whitman's prose at this time became more literary in its derivations: "Bervance: or, Father and Son," for example, is a Poesque psychic melodrama about a father who commits his son to a madhouse, though the son is not mad; "A Legend of Life and Love" is a moral allegory in the manner of Hawthorne. One of the first productions of Whitman as a literary critic is a piece called "Boz and Democracy," published in 1842 in *Brother Jonathan*; this is a defense of Dickens against the charge that he is too realistic and writes too much of evil and degradation; Whitman asserts that Dickens is "wholesome" and "a true democratic writer." The influence of Dickens is dimly to be seen in Whitman's most ambitious effort at prose fiction, his temperance tract of 1842 called *Franklin Evans: or The Inebriate*. This short novel is an outrageous piece of vulgarity and was written as hack work by an author who had already lost some of his earlier prudery but not, we may think, his solidly entrenched personal abstemiousness. Whitman said in 1888 of *Franklin Evans*, "It was damned rot . . . not insincere, perhaps, but rot." He liked to say that he had written it in three days "with the help of a bottle of port or what not." Perhaps there was a bottle of port (or, as someone else remembered, a series of gin cocktails), but the visions of the drunken newspaperman writing a hack work on temperance which Whitman's words evoke is certainly as mythical as many of the other images by which this romancer and poseur represented himself.*

The foppish Walt soon began to give way to the more simply clad but still elegant man of affairs with his copious beard and wide-brimmed hat who turned up, in 1846, as the editor of the *Brooklyn Eagle*. Salutary changes were taking place, in the early 1840's, in Whitman's personality. These were mirrored to some extent in his writing, which begins to show a new capacity to emerge from the smothering fantasies of the unhappy adolescent into an air which, if not exactly open, is nevertheless capable of sustaining a further range of life. The tautness of the dandy, like the grip which prudery and fear of experience had upon the young man, begins to relax. And it is in this period that one of Whitman's most famous characteristics begins fully to manifest itself: his capacity, that is, for absorbing experience, for observing and

* The book was truly "rot," however, as the following example of narrative style will suggest:

"There were four of us. The leader of the gang, who was addressed as Picaroon, had several weapons about his person that were evidently capable of doing dangerous work.

" 'Come, lads,' said he, 'the business we are on will be none the worse for a few glasses. Let us drink.'

"At the word, we helped ourselves, and tossed the liquor down our throats."

Such passages as this, together with others of sententious moralizing, are more entertaining than the implausible story of the innocent young hero's narrow escape from the sink of iniquity.

reporting the mere myriad sights and sounds of things. In these years his "passion for ferries" flowered, as well as his love of "omnibus jaunts and drivers" and "plays and operas too." Such impressions as those of Broadway, which he recorded in *Specimen Days*, helped to put Whitman more widely and deeply in touch with life, helped to furnish out the moral abstractions and fantasies of his mind with concrete meanings, or to banish them altogether.

Whitman was editor of the *Brooklyn Eagle* from March 1846 to January 1848. The *Eagle* was a flourishing paper which purveyed the attitudes of the Democratic party to the rapidly growing city. Whitman soon became a civic figure as well as a well-known editor. He attended meetings, marched in parades, was made a member of the Fourth of July Celebration Committee, and served as a political functionary. As editor and citizen he attended church services, Sunday school picnics, plays, art exhibits, and concerts. In after years Whitman remembered his job on the *Eagle* as one of the easiest and most pleasant "sits" he had ever had. And indeed, though he probably did more work than he liked to remember, his daily schedule does not sound onerous. He wrote his editorials in the morning, left the office for a walk or lunch, and returned in the afternoon to read proof. Later in the afternoon he habitually went to Gray's Swimming Bath; a former printer's devil remembered years afterward that it had been his custom to accompany Walt to the bath and to pump the water for the editor's shower. The editor often completed his day with a ferry trip to New York, a ride on the horsecars, or a visit to an opera or play.

Whitman's editorials for the *Eagle* are not distinguished; usually they seem desultory or impromptu. That the same is true of his writings for the *Brooklyn Times* (1857–59) proves the inadvisability of taking the *Eagle* editorials as evidence in any account of the development of Whitman's genius. There are certain superficial relationships of theme and attitude between the editorials and the poetry, but far more striking is the almost total impossibility of predicting the poetry, in any exact literary sense, from the editorials. A few of the editorials are interesting, however, as bearing on the poet's life and opinions. His political ideas were Democratic, verging later upon the Free Soil position. But I wish to refer here to only two aspects of the *Eagle* editorials: their strain of sentimentality and their view of European literature.

Perhaps Whitman's most amusing editorials are those in which he praises the domestic virtues. How fortunate is that home, he says, where one finds "real quiet enjoyment—the true coy comfort, that loves to nestle in quiet." And how praiseworthy are the novels of Fredrika Bremer, wherein we are taught "the mild virtues—how charity and forebearance and love are potent in the domestic circle . . . how indulgence in stormy passions leads invariably to sorrow—and depicting in especial the character of *a good, gentle mother*. . . . If we ever have children," concludes the editorialist, they will read, first, the New Testament, and second, Miss Bremer. This sentimental piety is not, one would gather, mere pretense. Although living at this time with his father and mother, Whitman was already embarked on his semi-Bohemian bachelor's career. But the feeling he exhibits in praising domesticity is one of the many indications that in his sentiments and, indeed, in his profoundest emotional disposition Whitman was conservative and nostalgic.

Whitman's literary nationalism was already established in his mind in the *Eagle* days. He attacks "servile imitation" and plumps for a genuine native literature. One must of course honor "the sweetness and majesty of Shakespeare, Goethe, and some of the Italian poets— the fiery breath of Byron, the fascinating melancholy of Rousseau, the elegance and candor of Hume and Gibbon." Yet the literature of Europe is incurably Tory, or, as he was to say in his later writings, "feudal." Whitman had always loved Scott, especially *The Heart of Midlothian* and the poetry. Yet the American reader must admit that Scott and Southey "exercise an evil influence" through their Toryism. And who must not deplore the "tinsel sentimentality of Bulwer," "the vulgar coarseness of Maryatt," "the dishwater senility of Lady Blessington," and "the nastiness of the French Paul De Kock"? "Shall Hawthorne," asks our rhetorician, "shiver with neglect while the public run after this foreign trash?"

We would gather from these editorials that fundamentally Whitman had two objections to European literature: it was undemocratic and it was heterosexual; it spoke of the world as if human beings were divided into classes and the sexes into male and female, and these divisions Whitman could not contemplate without feeling that they were in some way unworthy. His own literary prophetic vision of ideal democracy provides for a world in which these "feudal" distinctions shall, in so far as may prove possible, disappear. The roots of his feeling about the literary treatment of sex are not to be found merely in his democratic credo of equality. They are, of course, neurotic, as will be seen from the fact that when he objects to "sentimentality" in literature, as in speaking of Bulwer, he is always speaking of erotic, heterosexual emotions; he is not objecting to sentimentality as such but to

sexuality as such, or at least to the representation of sexuality in literature when this representation is given even the slightest erotic color.
This is not at odds with Whitman's poems about sex, such as *Children
of Adam* and the *Calamus* poems, which, as has often been observed, do
not speak of heterosexuality except in the most remote and abstract
language.

The problem of Whitman's sexuality has been strongly connected
by most biographers with the "New Orleans episode." Whitman was
in New Orleans, working on a newspaper called the *Crescent*, from
February to May of 1848. With the possible exception of one or two
later trips to the South, this was the only extensive journey Whitman
made before he published *Leaves of Grass* (he returned from New
Orleans, however, by way of the Mississippi, the Great Lakes, Niagara,
and the Hudson).

Enticed by the combination of deliberate suppression of fact and
the carefully nurtured air of mystery with which Whitman always
spoke of his New Orleans venture, some biographers have wanted to
see in it the critical moment of his career, although one might more
properly believe that for a man of Whitman's organic constitution there
can hardly be any one experience upon which his whole life may be said
to turn. Whitman was not a man to go from critical experience to
critical experience. Rather his life might be called an evasion according to plan. He evaded everything he could, from the pursuits of the
workaday world to those isolated religious, imaginative, or sexual experiences which become critical episodes in the lives of other poets.
As Whitman himself instinctively knew, his poetic genius would not
be liberated by a startling experience, by a ravishing dream, by a vision
of God, or by love for a woman or man. It would be self-liberated like
leaves of grass, slowly, painfully, and in due time, after its long dor-
mancy.

Holloway's *Whitman, An Interpretation in Narrative* was one
of the semipopular "Freudian" biographies of the 1920's, and the emphasis it makes on the New Orleans episode may be taken as typical
of a whole school of biographers (although, as one may think, a genu-
inely Freudian view of Whitman's life might lead to conclusions different from Holloway's). There being no indisputable evidence that
Walt Whitman became involved with one or more women in New
Orleans, the biographers have had to content themselves with putting together scraps of dubious evidence. Most arresting of these is
Whitman's letter to John Addington Symonds, written at Camden in
1890, wherein the poet's would-be disciple was told: "My life, young

manhood, mid-age, times South, etc., have been jolly bodily, and doubtless open to criticism. Though unmarried I have had six children—
two are dead—one living Southern grandchild, fine boy, writes to me
occasionally—circumstances (connected with their fortune and benefit) have separated me from intimate relations." Although the burden
of proof would seem to be on Whitman or on his six children, one cannot say with absolute certainty that his statement is pure fabrication.
Yet on the whole the presumption is that the "six children" were
invented by an old man who wished to call off the dogs of a young
idealist bent on securing from him an admission that the *Calamus*
poems might be taken as the bible of homosexual love. One may
guess that Whitman, weak and tired in 1890, may have taken what he
thought to be the quickest way to scotch the rather involved and Pla-
tonized homosexual idealism of writers like Symonds, in so far as they
tried to derive it from *Leaves of Grass*. Clearly the imputation worried, confused, and annoyed him.

The other scraps of "evidence" for the New Orleans sexual experience are much less striking than the letter to Symonds. There is, for
example, the sketch called "A Night at the Terpsichore Ball" published
in the *Crescent* (a story telling how the author got himself introduced
to a beautiful and cultivated lady by a man who later turns out to be
her husband—but this sounds like standard popular humor, not autobiography). There is another piece in the *Crescent* defending nude
statuary (what a momentous loss to civilization that Whitman and
Hawthorne did not engage in a dialogue on this matter!). There is
Whitman's knowledgeable description of the New Orleans octoroons—
"women with splendid bodies, no bustles, no corsets, no enormities of
any sort; large luminous bright eyes; face a rich olive; habits indolent,
yet not lazy as we define laziness North; always more than pretty—
'pretty' is too weak a word to apply to them." The poem "Once I
Pass'd Through a Populous City," which contains the line "Yet now
of all that city I remember only a woman I casually met there who
detain'd me for love of me," was often cited as referring to New Orleans
and lending credibility to Whitman's connection with a woman, until
it was discovered that in another, earlier version of the poem the poet
spoke of himself as being detained not by a "woman" but a "man."

The arguments for "the New Orleans woman" have often taken a
purely literary turn. Holloway, for example, saw in Whitman's visit
to New Orleans a pilgrimage of the naïve Northerner to the Paris of
the South. In New Orleans "Whitman had found himself akin, through
the flesh, with all mankind"; and this broadening of experience had a

liberating effect so that, as Holloway suggested, "the floodgates of a highly sexed nature, the 'pent-up rivers' of himself gave way, and Whitman returned to nature" (as we worldlings of the 'fifties return to the vivid biographers of the 'twenties). Behind the scenes of this drama of self-transcendence there lurks a shadowy octoroon, to be compared with Shakespeare's Dark Lady and Melville's Fayaway.

It is difficult to think of Whitman as having "a highly sexed nature." We are not bound, either, to believe that even if he did have a woman or women in New Orleans or elsewhere, this would have been a critical event in his life. If in some sense the hypothetical experience might be regarded as crucial, there is good reason for thinking that it gave Whitman, or confirmed in him, a basic feeling of remoteness from women, rather than leading him to a new connection with life and nature.

The facts known at present about Whitman seem to accord with a very diffusely, rather than a highly, sexed nature. There is considerable evidence to show that he may have made connections with both sexes, although none of it is conclusive. He was in person bisexual, his body being large and sturdy but without any apparent musculature beneath the soft feminine flesh. There seems no doubt that he had inclinations in both directions—whether or not there ever was a "Washington woman" or New Orleans octoroon or a series of young stage drivers or Civil War veterans like his friend Pete Doyle. We find a number of cryptic jottings in his notebooks of 1868–70, for example, which suggest a confused and hectic sexual versatility. *"Pursue her no more,"* he admonishes himself (this passage does not seem to be mere phrenological jargon, as has been maintained). Again he writes, "Depress the adhesive nature . . . It is in excess—making life a torment." This *is* phrenological jargon, "adhesive" referring to the comradely love of males. That he had at times a homosexual sensibility is shown by a letter he wrote to some of his New York companions during the Washington days: "Only I have some curious yarns I promise you my darlings & gossips, by word of mouth whene're we meet. . . .

"I remain yet much of the old vagabond that so gracefully becomes me. I miss you my darlings & gossips, Fred Gray, & Bloom and Russell and everybody. . . .

"My health, strength, personal beauty, etc., are, I am happy to inform you, without diminution, but on the contrary quite the reverse. I weigh full 220 pounds avoirdupois. Yet still retain my usual perfect shape—a regular model."

Perhaps the best supposition about Whitman is that he was sexually versatile, that he was more strongly drawn to men than to women, but that probably his life was not overtly and actually sexual at all, since he always found ways of converting his sexual impulses to artistic ends or generalizing them into a vague, diffuse, and psychically infantile feeling of "comradeship."

To conclude the New Orleans episode, it would be wrong to discount altogether its influence on Whitman's development. It must indeed have had some strong effect on a young man who had already manifested an extraordinary capacity for obsorbing experience, for taking in the sights and sounds of the world with a unique sense of wonder and freshness. There were experiences to be had in New Orleans in 1848, besides that of making a mistress of an octoroon. Unfortunately, we do not know much of what Walt did in New Orleans—*Specimen Days*, in which he records at least something of what was memorable in his life, mentions his days on the *Crescent* only in passing. But we do know (from his newspaper articles) that he had seen new vistas, observed new types, exposed his omnivorous sensibility to a new part of the world, seen depths of degradation and manifestations of colorful temperament unknown in Brooklyn. In the language of *Song of Myself*, it was a new advance in "identification," in drawing into the self the experience of the world.

There is little to record of the years between 1848 and 1855. Whitman's career as a journalist at this time seems even more inconsequential and subject to misfortune than in previous years; and one has the sense, if only from the dearth of information, that the really meaningful and exciting events of Whitman's life were now interior, where the hesitant but restless "embryons" of *Leaves of Gross* were stirring. The most auspicious outward event was his becoming editor, soon after his return from New Orleans, of a new paper in Brooklyn called the *Freeman*. He was appropriately hailed by a rival paper which announced that "Rienzi has returned . . . our old Barnburner friend himself." As the name indicates, the editorial policy of the new paper was to be Free Soil. But the plant where the *Freeman* was printed burned down on the night of the first issue, and although Whitman was able to resume publication after two months, the times were not propitious for the venture, the Free Soil party being, for one thing, on its way to rejoining the regular party. After a year Whitman left the paper, with an editorial assurance that he was grateful to his friends and associates, and concluding: "My enemies—and old Hunkers generally—I disdain and defy the same as ever.—Walter Whitman." Between 1849 and 1851 Whitman, besides doing free-lance writing and perhaps compositing, maintained an unsuccessful printing office and store in a building whose second floor was inhabited for a time by his father's family. Walt's brother George remembered that in these years Walt had not worked regularly, that he rose late, did a lot of reading, and wrote a great deal, mostly lectures as the family thought, though, as George said, "we did not know what he was writing." Even less eventful were the years between 1851 and 1854. It was then that Walt took to carpentering with his father and achieved his final transformation, as Perry remarked, from the young dandy to the "quiet, slow-footed, grey-bearded working man." One has occasional glimpses of activities later to be productive of poetry—Whitman's habit of reading Emerson's essays during the lunch hour, for instance, and his reading of Homer, Sophocles, Shakespeare, the Bible, and Epictetus (a lifelong favorite). He seems also to have spent a part of every summer wandering about rural Long Island, whose country influences he always found so profoundly restful and recruiting, as well as instinct with moral and poetic qualities.

Whitman was one of those writers who, like Mark Twain, Shaw, Dostoevski, and Yeats, present themselves through their art or their public life in the guise of more than one self. (In his notebook Whitman had written, perhaps as early as 1847, "I cannot understand the mystery, but I am always conscious of myself as two." And he provisionally identified the "two" as "my soul and I.") Invoking the Dionysian rites and the Aristophanic comedy, Nietzsche asserted the necessity of the double personality. "Everything that is profound loves the mask," he wrote; "the profoundest things have a hatred even of figure and likeness. Should not the *contrary* be the right disguise for the shame of a God to go about in?" Like other modern writers Whitman found it temperamentally pleasurable as well as strategically necessary to interpose a half-ironic image of himself between the world and that profound part of his personality which hated figure and likeness—the unconscious mind with its spontaneous, lawless, poetic impulses. He invented not one but several public personalities—the worldly, dandified young metropolitan journalist of the early 1840's; the homely, Christlike carpenter and radical of the early 1850's; the full-bearded, sunburned, clean-limbed, vigorously sexed, burly common man of the later 'fifties and early 'sixties; the male nurse and good gray poet of the Washington period; the sage of Camden of the late years.

In having contrived so striking a procession of public images (actually all but the young journalist dandy are aspects of one large public gesture), Whitman is unique among American writers. The masks interest us only because we see that they are not assumed merely to fool the public. There was, to be sure, a certain strain of "insincerity" in Whitman. He wrote anonymous panegyrics of *Leaves of Grass* and generally puffed his own writings when he got the chance. He allowed early biographies of himself to be published (he even collaborated more or less in their composition) which contained misleading information: such as that the author of *Leaves of Grass* had, by 1855, traveled throughout the United States and, therefore, knew at firsthand the geographical phenomena the poems celebrate. Yet without wishing to condone dishonesty, one may suggest that modern Americans are far too sensitive about sincerity—except in personal relationships, it is after all one of the minor virtues. Whitman may have gone off the deep end in pursuit of "sympathy" and "comradeship," but at least he does not come bounding up to us with that doglike guilelessness our contemporary culture admires. He wore the mask of the "American humorist"; he was quirky, ironic, "indirect," guileful. As he remarked to Edward Carpenter, one of his English admirers, "There is something in my nature *furtive* like an old hen! . . . Sloane Kennedy [another disciple] calls me 'artful'—which about hits the mark."

Whitman was a "democratic" version of that modern personality adumbrated in the *Rameau's Nephew* of Diderot—the divided, multiple personality, a shifting amalgam of sycophancy and sloth, of mimetic brilliance and Dionysian inspiration, of calculating common sense and philosophic insight, of raffish Bohemianism, of Rousseauistic disorientation and primitivism—a mind neurotic, lonely, unstable, libidinous, envious, indolent, suffused with yeasty eruptions from the unconscious depths, turning uncertainly from self-assertion to self-recrimination and despair, brooding with the same sense of mystery on the most sublime and the most vulgar and sordid aspects of life.

As I say, one is not for long touched or interested by a writer's public poses when these are too preponderantly fake—as in the case of Oscar Wilde. The poses, we feel, must be largely a necessity induced in the writer by his own personality or by the culture he lives in. Certainly they were so induced in Whitman.

Looked at as a matter of "public relations," the problem is simple. Whitman was a poet of a very advanced and difficult sort; he was of dubious sex. This gave him two wars to fight with the advancing bourgeois America of his time, and two wars to fight with himself, so much a part was he of this America, so much did he share in its tastes and believe in its moral proscriptions. The culture of his time admired (much more so than our culture does today) the prophet, the orator, the sententious democratic reformer; and it admired rough plebeian masculinity. It would condone oddity of behavior (more so than now) so long as the main requirements were met. Whitman met them. When he discovered how strong was the public condemnation of sex in literature Whitman added to the façade the "good gray poet" (or gratefully allowed it to be added by his disciple and apologist, O'Connor). These poses are, of course, involved extensively in Whitman's poetry, a large portion of *Leaves of Grass* being little more than a rhetorical proclamation of them. From the point of view of art and under the aspect of eternity the public figure and his democratic program (valuable as these are in themselves) were the massive irrelevance and waste required for the indulgence of the essential Whitman—the young comic god and profound elegist.

Whitman had it somewhat easier than Melville or Mark Twain. Neurotic, riven, and vividly paradoxical as his personality was, many of the conflicting elements were subsumable under his monumental inertia and placidity, which allowed him to live more at rest than they in nineteenth-century America. The battle of Melville and Mark Twain with their times, though not more fundamental than that of Whitman, was more violent and more wearing. One might find a genetic explanation for this in the fact that all three had rather unstable fathers who "failed," but that whereas Melville and Mark Twain had mothers who were inclined to be harsh and morally overbearing and for whom they came to have very equivocal feelings, Whitman's mother was what is supposed to be the American male's ideal—she was firm, patient, hard-working, sympathetic and loving, and she lived on in her son. One may note by way of parenthesis that, after making all due allowances for those differences which have led many critics to place Walt Whitman and Henry James at opposite poles in the history of American culture, from the point of view of psychic development Whitman can be thought of as a kind of plebeian James. Both idolized their mothers as the essence of beautiful maternity; both bore the same names as their strong, radical, but unstable fathers; both tended ambivalently to identify themselves with their fathers, in attitudes alternately submissive (as when Walt became a carpenter) and hostile; both were rather passive and moody second sons; both patently overcame their feelings of powerlessness and femininity in their writing, as James did with his vision of the power and glory of European culture and as Whitman did by allying himself with the vast energy of nineteenth-century America; both returned mystically to their own sense of being wounded and unfitted for life by identifying with the sick and dying, as they both did by visiting wounded veterans of that Civil War in which neither directly engaged. James himself commemorated this shared experience by remembering in later years that his visits to the convalescent troops in Rhode Island had been paralleled by "dear old Walt"; and adding that "I like to treat myself to making out that I can scarce have brought to the occasion . . . less of the consecrating sentiment than he."

In effect Whitman was cannier than Melville or Twain. His battle was more covert, more "furtive"; his essential genius was buried deep in his massive, slow-moving personality, showed itself on few occasions (not at all until he was thirty-six), masked itself behind a consistent and extensive series of public gestures, and quickly disappeared altogether. Despite the relative failure of *Leaves of Grass*, Whitman did not suffer the long nervous exacerbations of Melville and Twain. One may note that Van Wyck Brooks was wrong to suggest, in *The Ordeal of Mark Twain*, that when Whitman retired to Camden in 1873, he was retreating like a whipped dog from a hostile and unappreciative America—this is the kind of speculation that invites the Philistine reply: "No, he went because he had a stroke and his brother George lived in Camden." I would add, however, that after nineteenth-century American culture has been recaptured in what plenitude it had (by writers like De Voto and Brooks himself), Brooks's biography of Twain seems still *essentially* right, although errant in many particulars. His book remains a classic in the study of the position of our great writers in the nineteenth century.

Sociologically speaking, Whitman's poses were the reflex of his culture. From the point of view of his art, they were the concerted maneuver which allowed him to produce a small body of great poetry. Psychologically speaking they were the ego ideals which sought to control an unruly unconscious, or to mediate between it and the world. If we turn to the difficult, and doubtless insoluble problem of explaining how, apparently almost overnight, Walt Whitman ceased being merely a desultory editor and carpenter and became a great poet, we will doubtless conclude that only a line of psychological speculation can avoid sententious irrelevancies. Of course it will not solve the "problem."

There is hardly any literary evidence which allows us to trace a development of either thought or style. The scanty notebooks, going back as early as 1847, are of little interest. The few scattered examples of Whitman's early poetry, extending from imitations of Scott to a broken versification dimly resembling that of *Leaves of Grass*, are of some technical interest. They raise the question—but hardly more—as to how Whitman achieved the language without which he would not have been a poet.

The three most frequently recurring explanations of Whitman's transformation from editor-carpenter to poet seem inadmissible. The first is that New Orleans and the octoroon Whitman met there converted the provincial Quakerish youth to life and liberated his creative powers. If we are right in thinking that Whitman was rather virginal than overtly sexual, we cannot give credence to the New Orleans explanation, in so far as this refers to a sexual connection. And in any case even so slow a personality as Whitman's would hardly require seven years (from 1848 to 1855) to exhibit the results of so momentous an experience.

A second explanation is that at some time after the New Orleans trip and subsequent adventures probably involving sexual attempts, Whitman had the tragic but purgative and liberating experience of recognizing and accepting the fact that he was homosexual. But here again the objection must be that Whitman's sexuality was so diffuse and sublimated that it could never have generated in him any definitive disposition or crucial recognition and acceptance of such a disposition. Furthermore, the evidence that Whitman had heterosexual relations is almost as substantial as the evidence that he was homosexual—and neither is *very* substantial.

A third explanation is that Whitman had a mystical experience, not necessarily involving sex, which gave him his characteristic vision, that at some crucial moment he was "illuminated" and perceived the universe in all its totality—"cosmic consciousness," Dr. Richard Bucke, one of the disciples and an alienist, called it. Observers as acute as Santayana and William James concluded that the essential quality of Whitman's mind was mysticism, although to the literary critic it does not seem so. Comparisons have been made between Whitman and the Oriental mystics; St. Paul and Rousseau, struck down by the apocalyptic influx of light, have been recalled. There may be sometimes a kind of mysticism at work in Whitman's poetry. But it is hardly ever distinguishable from merely vague thought and diffuse metaphor—and, therefore, it seems more gratuitous or honorific than accurate to refer to it as mysticism. But from a literary point of view this "mysticism" is surely not characteristic. And in fact the more one reviews the evidence and the more one reads the poems, the less likely does the "mystical experience" seem and the less relevant to an understanding of such poems as *Song of Myself* does it become, even if it occurred. As we have noted before there is no evidence about Whitman which encourages us to think him capable of any stern, overwhelming, or intense spiritual experience. Except in his poems, his mind and emotions were not grasping, imperious and rapid like those of St. Paul or Rousseau, nor capable of the disciplined masochism of the Oriental mystic. Whitman made the right analogy: he was like the grass, he was a "slow arriver," his poetic powers emerged gradually and painfully, and whatever definitive redispositions there were were secret and subliminal but of the native soil.

Furthermore, it seems a matter of general principle that poetic experience, although it may include it, cannot be equated with or produced by mystic experience, properly so called. Mysticism leads to the ecstatic contemplation of the naught; it does not of itself produce poetry, which is a metaphorical construction of the aught. Poetry is made by the imagination, and, as Santayana insists, the life of reason depends on our ability to distinguish between the imaginative and the mystic (although he himself failed to do so in his attack on Whitman). I do not wish to deny the usefulness of the word "mysticism" in speaking of the general tenor of Whitman's mind, but only to doubt its relevance to the strictly literary question and to the question of his emergence as a poet.

A more convincing line of speculation as to how Whitman became a poet probably has to begin with the theory developed by Jean Catel in his *Walt Whitman: La Naissance du Poète* (1929), a much more solid piece of Freudian analysis than Holloway's. With Catel one notes the morose, disorganized personality of Walt's father, the anxious instability of the family as it moved from house to house, the unfolding fate of Walt's brothers and sisters which, as we have noted, was to be on the whole a story of sickness, depravity, and insanity—when Alcott visited Whitman in 1856 he found that Walt shared a bed with his twenty-one-year-old brother Eddie, the imbecile and epileptic. One observes the uncertainty of Whitman's life as a young man, after he had emerged from what the poet himself called his "unhappy" boyhood. From the time Walt began to work in printing shops up until 1855, and thereafter for that matter, his career consisted of a series of advances and retreats, of abortive attempts to hold jobs, to become a writer of editorials, sketches, and short stories. One postulates the failure and pain of the young man's sexual experiments, the anxiety consequent upon his gradual realization of his bisexuality and his autoeroticism—the "I" in *Song of Myself* has two aspects or voices: the wistful, lonely, hurt, feminine, erotically demanding voice, which alternates with that of the bearded, sunburned, masculine, democratic "rough." And the poem contains passages, of course, which are frankly autoerotic.

The emergence of Whitman's genius may be understood as the consequence of his having failed, because of neurotic disturbances, to make terms with the world. In the early 1850's he found a compensatory way of dealing with a world which threatened to defeat him. If he could not subdue it on its own terms, he would do so by committing himself entirely to that rich fantasy life of which he felt himself increasingly capable. (That Whitman conceived of his own poetic emergence in a way that substantiates the present argument is shown by his remark that "the *Democratic Review* essays and tales came from the surface of the mind, and had no connection with what lay below— a great deal of which indeed was below consciousness. At last came the time when the concealed growth had to come to light.") His power of fantasy would allow him to escape into an innocent, regressive, Eden-like realm and it would also allow him symbolically to assault and overwhelm a world of ordinary reality which had proved to be, on its own terms, too much for him. He would utterly escape and defy the world's attempt to establish in his shifting psychic economy a superego—to impose upon him this or that conventional "identity." He would allow his unconscious the freedom it demanded. He would free the ego of all prudential considerations, and make it dance to the tune of the unconscious. He would write a poem full of the sense of release and novelty, redolent with the uncanny unpredictableness of images fresh from the subliminal mind, and the subject of the poem would be the self— that is, the unconscious mind—"the infinite and omnigenous" self and it would describe the self as a timeless universal continuum but also as having the capacity to advance and retreat, to merge with and to extricate itself at will from any and all "identities." The poem would be full of philosophy and high thought, to be sure, but it would purvey the philosophy in a style determined by the sheer solipsism and incongruity of unconscious thought.

So free and aggressive an assertion of unconscious impulse might be expected to generate a good deal of guilt. And this will account in part for the rather extensive revisions Whitman made of *Song of Myself* in later editions, carefully excising or rewording sections which spoke too frankly of such matters as adolescent sexual confusions. It will account for his deliberate silence about what he was doing in the period just before 1855; and it gives us a lead toward explaining the whole elaborate evasion which constituted his public pose and which he fostered and condoned in the early biographies. Whitman was by no means always the free spirit he was in *Song of Myself*. Taking him by and large, he was canny and prudential. In an early notebook he had written that to be an American "is to be illimitably proud, independent, self-possessed, generous, and gentle. It is to accept nothing except what is equally free and eligible to anybody else. It is to be poor rather than rich—but to prefer death sooner than any mean dependence. —Prudence is part of it, because prudence is the right arm of independence." Nothing could be more characteristic of Whitman than that last sentence. It reminds one of his amusing exhortation to Traubel in later years: "Be radical, be radical, be not too damn radical."

The analysis of Whitman's personality set forth in the last paragraphs cannot, of course, fully account for Whitman the poet. It is impossible to say why, given his psychic difficulties, he became a poet and not (like his brother Jesse) a psychotic case, except that he had "genius." On a historical view, however, one notices a happy conjunction of forces, involving Whitman's emerging personality and the assumptions of the culture he lived in, partly as Whitman instinctively understood and shared them, partly as he found them rationalized and given a language in the essays of Emerson.

In order to arrive at the vision of things which we find in *Song of Myself* the self had to be apprehended as a felt presence, as an idea, and as a metaphor or conceit. It had to be identified with the unconscious at least completely enough so that it would take to itself some of the powers and qualities of the unconscious. But first (the chronology is, of course, for purposes of discussion only) Whitman had to liberate within himself and become aware of his unconscious mind in its poetry-making aspect. That he had done this by 1855 is shown by another poem which appeared in the first edition, *The Sleepers*. This poem is of interest to the psychological investigator because of its presentation of the dream activity of the mind as the way in which universal equality and love are achieved, the way in which joy and vitality are released, and, most important, the way in which the poetic imagination learns to operate.

Given the unconscious so conceived, what was needed before *Song of Myself* could be written was the idea of the self and some reason for connecting the self with the unconscious. Several things forced the self upon Whitman's attention. He was characteristically, as he said, conscious of himself as "two" (psychologically perhaps the result of his bisexual nature). The democracy of which Whitman was so natively a part exalted the free, self-sufficient individual, having lost under the impact of Jeffersonian and Jacksonian theories much of whatever sense of traditional, institutional life and the place of the individual therein it had once possessed. The Quaker tendency of the Whitman family enhanced the sense of the inner mystery. Transcendentalist theory made the self a godlike power—omniscient, omnipresent, omnipotent.

In "Self-Reliance" Emerson mythicized the self in a way which could hardly fail to have the most conclusive and electric effect on a mind such as Whitman's. "What [asked Emerson] is the aboriginal self, on which a universal reliance may be grounded? . . . The inquiry leads us to that source, at once the essence of genius, of virtue, and of life, which we call spontaneity or instinct. We denote this primary wisdom as intuition, whilst all later teachings are tuitions. In that deep force, the last fact behind which analysis cannot go, all things find their common origin."

Taking a psychological view of this characteristic formulation (as the references to spontaneity, instinct, and the "deep force" of the mind allow us to do), we understand Emerson to say that an inquiry into the self, both in its individual and universal aspects, leads us to the unconscious part of the mind. In another sense, Emerson is apparently saying that the self, considered as "aboriginal," *is* the unconscious, that in its aboriginal aspect, it not only leads us to the unconscious—to the "last fact behind which analysis cannot go"—it *is* this "last fact." One need not find Emerson's words perfectly clear as psychology or metaphysics to see in them a remarkably suggestive poetic metaphor. And it must certainly have been as such that the formulation appealed to Whitman. In this basic metaphor Emerson can be said to have made connections among the self or "identity," the unconscious, and the universal, and to have given the whole vision the status of "wisdom" in just such a manner as would precipitate a similar crystallization in the mind of Whitman. All the elements were in Whitman, the products of his peculiar temperament and of his democratic surroundings. But it was from Emerson that he first sensed how they might be put together and embodied in words.

LESLIE A. FIEDLER

Images of Walt Whitman

It is difficult to remember that *Leaves of Grass* is, in its conception at least, an anonymous poem. Even its author seems more than once in the course of thirty years of revision to have forgotten that fact; and certainly he became convinced before the end of his life that it was a guilty secret, to be hidden with all the resources of a furtiveness of which he liked to boast. The signed proem, the endless insistence upon the first person, the deliberate confusion of the Mask and the self—all these come to conceal the truth which the authorless title page of the first edition confesses: that the "Walt Whitman" of *Leaves of Grass* is a persona really created by the poems it fictionally creates. An "eidolon" Whitman preferred to call it in his own highfalutin vocabulary, an "avatara," or more simply, "My Fancy." At the end of his life, he confesses under this name the doubleness of image and self:

> Good-bye my Fancy!
> Farewell dear mate, dear love!
> I'm going away, I know not where,
> Or to what fortune, or whether I may ever see you again,
> So Good-bye my Fancy.

It is his farewell to his truest love, cherished with a passion beyond "amativeness" or "adhesiveness," and he will not admit finally that even dying can sever them.

> Yet let me not be too hasty,
> Long indeed have we lived, slept, filter'd, become really blended
>   into one;
> Then if we die we die together, (yes, we'll remain one,) . . .
> May-be it is yourself now really ushering me to the true songs,
>   (who knows?)
> May-be it is you the mortal knob really undoing, turning . . .

There is the real romantic madness in this (and the metaphysics which lies beyond it), the irrational conviction that made Balzac cry out on his deathbed for a doctor of his own inventing, and which leads Whitman to dream that he and his fictive "Walt" will share all eternity.

But we must not let the final metaphysics blind us to the initial assumption upon which the wit and pathos of the poems really depend. Emerson, who felt so deeply into *Leaves of Grass* in his first reading, knew its namelessness, realized that the poem's "Walt Whitman" could not really exist. "I did not know until I last night saw the book advertised in a newspaper that I could trust the name as real and available for a post-office," he wrote to Whitman; but he let the newspaper fact convince him, and opened a correspondence that could only end in comedy and equivocation. It was not, of course, "Walt" who answered but "Walt's" promoter, rubbing his hands together and bowing like a salesman over his shoddy goods. "Master, I am a man who has perfect faith. Master, we have not come through centuries, tastes, heroisms, fables to halt in this land today. . . ."

It sounds like an impersonation, even a parody, and in a sense it is. Later, Whitman was to learn to play his own eidolon with more conviction in reviews, introductions, and conversation; but never, except in his most intense poetic moments, could he help somehow travestying the beloved Fancy that possessed him only when it would. I do not share an admiration for Whitman's prose, which has for me generally the sense of pushing, thrusting—being by brute force Walt Whitman. The comparison suggests itself to the medium who feels obliged to fake at blank moments the real experience that fails him.

It is Whitman's own fault (and that of the disciples whom he suffered only too willingly) that metaphors of table tapping and the Beyond come so readily to our minds. One does not become a child of nature in the nineteenth century by attempting to eschew culture; one becomes, in so far as he fails, a *literary* version of the child of nature; and in so far as he succeeds, a creature of subculture: of the world of "cosmic consciousness" and phrenology that lurks beneath the surface of ideas proper. In the latter sense, Whitman is the Mary Baker Eddy of American poetry; in the former, he is its Ossian; and it is upon the literary analogy that I want to insist in order to redeem him from animal magnetism to art.

Ossian and Chatterton, the examples of the faked antique, the artificial "natural," of the higher hoax as Romantic poetry, suggest themselves; and Ossian, at least, Whitman has confessed to feeling as a temptation to be resisted. Whitman has actually much in common with such poets, especially the sense (one suspects) that the seeming fraud is the real truth, that the writer is truly possessed by the spirit he seems to invent, but also the anonymity prompted by both the desire to take in the reader and to establish the higher truth of the impersonation. In the Ossianic poet only the fictive singer is real; it is McPherson who does not exist—and if there is no forger there can be no forgery. Whitman has the advantage, to be sure, of playing a contemporary role, so that he is free to drop the cumbersome device of the "translated" or "discovered" manuscript—and has only to become in public life the person he invents, that is to say, to counterfeit himself rather than the text.

It is tempting to the stern moralist to see Whitman as the tragic victim of his own imposture. As the years and editions went by, the name "Walt Whitman" crept from its place in the poem to the spine of the book; and the anonymous author almost irrecoverably disappeared, lying, distorting, destroying all evidence of any life outside the legend. Even his face changed, along with his stance and costume, as he willed himself from photograph to photograph into the image of the Rowdy, the Christ, the Workman's Friend, the Beard and the Butterfly, the Good Gray Poet. The one portrait of the anonymous author, an indolent dandy with a pert beardlet, shocks us. We tend to believe only what the poem tells us, that Walt never dressed in black, that he is

> Of pure American breed, of reckless health, his body perfect,
> free from taint from top to toe, free forever from headache
> and dyspepsia, clean-breathed
> Ample-limbed, a good feeder . . . bearded, calm, unrefined . . .

The unexpected revelations of the autopsy: "the left suprarenal capsule tubercular . . . a cyst the size of a pigeon's egg," or the glimpses in the accounts of early acquaintances of the shy misfit who drank only water and was never "bothered up" by a woman, these affect us like slander: nature slandering art, the actual the mythical.

But Whitman was finally the master of the actual, achieving by sheer will the Mask he dreamed. It is revealing to see him through the letters of *The Wound-Dresser*, walking the wards of the Washington hospitals during the Civil War: oppressed by headaches, worried about his weight, fussing like an old grandmother with his jars of jam, secretly titillated by all those beautiful young men so touchingly maimed; and yet somehow *really* exuding the strength and health he did not possess, convincing and helping others by his mythic powers;

and paying for it all finally, paying for the legend of absolute participation, the boast : "I was there !"

By the time he had invented the Good Gray Poet, he had burned
away all of himself that was not the image. "The secret" at which he
eternally hinted was now untellable ; perhaps he had actually forgotten
it. With the death of his mother, the anonymous poet (who had been,
above all, that mother's boy) was dead ; and Whitman's subsequent
paralysis was a declaration, as it were, that his body was now quite
simply the book—to be slipped into the blouses of young men, to lie
next to their flesh in innocence.

> Or if you will, thrusting me beneath your clothing,
> Where I may feel the throbs of your heart or rest upon your
>   hip . . .

The poem had become a man, but the man in turn had become the
poem. If this is a "pose" or "fraud," it is not one which we can despise.

No, if we are uncomfortable these days with Walt Whitman, it
is not because he pretended to be what he was not ; our judgments are
not so simple. "Above all to thine own self be true" was good enough
advice in the mind of one surer than we are what *is* the self. It is because the motives of his masquerade were so literary and conventional,
and the image of the poet he proposed himself such a ragbag of *Ver-
sunkenekulturgüte*, Rousseau, Goethe, George Sand, Carlyle, Emerson, and God knows what else, eked out with phrenology and Fourth
of July rhetoric, that we hesitate to accept him. If Whitman were
really the monster of health and sympathy he paints himself, really
the solemn discoverer of a New Sex or even of a hypostasized America
as his early followers came to believe, we should not abide him for a
moment. It is the poet who feared literature, the sly old maid finally
trapped by his own cunning who is *our* Whitman ; and the point of *our
Leaves of Grass* lies precisely in the distance between the poet and his
eidolon. If that distance did not exist, Whitman would have been
laughed out of existence by the first sophomore who snickered at
"I dote on myself, there is that lot of me and all so luscious . . ."

I remember not many years ago a black-bordered notice in *Furioso*,
advising certain rejected contributors that Walt Whitman was dead!
And it is true that *a* Walt Whitman, a series of Walt Whitmans, has
been destroyed, leaving only the poet we were not sure for a while was
there at all : the poet who peers slyly from behind his most portentous
statements to tip us the wink :

> To begin with take warning, I am surely different from what
>   you suppose ;

> Do you suppose you will find in me your ideal? . . .
> Do you think I am trusty and faithful?
> Do you see no further than this façade, this smooth and tolerant
>   manner of me?
> Do you suppose yourself advancing on real ground toward a
>   real heroic man?

or who, in double irony, speaks as the persona doubting the reality of the Whitman who creates it: "that shadow my likeness" who goes "chattering, chaffering" about the business of earning a living. "How often," remarks the poetic image coolly, "I question and doubt whether that is really me." The continual trifling with the illusion in *Leaves*, the ambiguity of the "I's" and the shifting irony of their confrontations ("O take my hand Walt Whitman! What do you hear Walt Whitman?"): this is far from the rant of a naïvely egoistic poet; it is a mannerist device, subtle and witty. To remember that *Leaves of Grass* is an anonymous poem is to notice that it is a humorous one!

This is a sense of Whitman long lost behind the constructions of those searching the poem for "a real heroic man," or hopefully taking its size for a guaranty of its epic qualities. But the lyrical impulse swollen to epic proportions (this is a discovery of our age) produces either conscious irony or unwitting absurdity. In Whitman there is much of both; the latter has been pointed out sufficiently by all but the most fervent apologists; the former has been noticed sympathetically in the past only by Constance Rourke. "At the same time he remained within a sphere which . . . had been defined in popular comedy, that of the acutely self-aware." Whitman was not unconscious of this, and his confession of his awareness should not be held against him as Esther Shephard has tried to do. "I pride myself on being a real humorist underneath everything else," he once remarked. And to someone who warned, "After all, you may end up as a comedian," he responded, "I might easily end up worse." And he did, poor Walt Whitman, he *did*! But this he foresaw, too.

> Nor will my poems do good only, they will do just as much evil,
>   perhaps more,
> For all is useless without that which you may guess at many
>   times and not hit, that which I hinted at . . .

Out of his image of himself, not only the living, wittily qualified eidolon of his best lines, but out of the ersatz of that eidolon provided by the poetry at its worst, out of ghostwritten adulatory reviews and memoirs there emerged a quadruple figure with a fictional life: The

Prophet of the New Era, the Faith Healer, the Sexual Emancipator, the Democrat at Home. The "hot, little" subprophets of the first generation, Burroughs and O'Connor and Bucke, soon detached the image of the Prophet, confronting lines from *Leaves* with lines from the Upanishads, suggesting a comparison with that other notable carpenter's son, Jesus; defining the state in which the Mask of Walt possessed the poet with Dr. Bucke's "Cosmic Consciousness"; in short, turning Whitman's poem into the scriptures of yet another homemade American religion. "Has our age produced a Christ—a Buddha? Has it given us a New Bible. I believe that in Walt Whitman we have the Prophet of a New Era, and that in his Leaves of Grass we have a book that will one day become a Bible to many seekers after light . . ." Within a generation the converts to the New Belief, the Whitmaniacs at large, had become a standard literary type. What had the poet done to deserve it?

Certainly, there is in him a vagueness, a failure to distinguish the poetic experience from the velleities that surround it, which blurs out into religiosity. It cannot be denied that Whitman wrote at times the sort of indeterminately ambitious verse that has been defined as "spilt religion"—and those to whom "spilt religion" is the only acceptable kind can hardly be blamed for finding in him evidences of their kind of sainthood. It must be said further, that Whitman exemplifies a modern mystery, a kind of "conversion" (or, perhaps, "possession," one scarcely knows what to call it), elsewhere found in Rousseau, in which a third-rate mind, sentimental, obtuse, and indolent, is illuminated with inexplicable suddenness by reading a phrenologist's report or the announcement of an essay contest in a local newspaper. But it is not the cosmos that inspires Rousseau or Whitman, not any Otherness—but precisely the dazzling vision of themselves. In their moments of ecstasy what is made flesh is not God but Jean Jacques or Walt.

Whitman as Christ has fared ill in our age that moves toward the poles of orthodoxy or unbelief, and from either pole regards the religioid with contempt. The image of the Source of Radiant Health has not done much better. The more intellectual turn to the analyst's couch or the orgone box for renewal, and the vulgar have their own non-literary prophets. What Mary Baker Eddy does not sufficiently cover ("I am he bringing help for the sick as they pant on their beds"), Dale Carnegie has claimed as his birthright ("Do you not see how it would serve to have such a body and soul that . . . everyone is impressed with your personality?").

In his role of Sexual Emancipator, however, Whitman has had a more successful career. About exactly what *kind* of emancipation Whitman promises there has been considerable disagreement, some finding in him the celebrator of paganism, a free heterosexual life; others (André Gide, for example) discovering comfort and reassurance for the homosexual, the normalizing of the abnormal; still others presenting him as the celebrator, if not the inventor, of what the Germans call the *Zwischenstufe*, what Edward Carpenter has translated as "the Intermediate Sex." As a deliverer of *verse* from sexual taboos, a forerunner of D. H. Lawrence, willing to be abused and abandoned to redeem the phallus and the orgasm to the imagination, Whitman deserves the credit he has been given. It is not, however, to the poems but to an image of Whitman that the legend of the Sexual Emancipator refers, to an image he himself sponsored of himself as the Defender of the Body against the overweening claims of the soul; as the Deliverer from Christianity with its antithesis of flesh and spirit and its distrust of passion; as the savior not of poetry but of *us*.

Those who would preserve this legend of Whitman as the spokesman for total physical love find themselves in the uncomfortable position of having to underestimate the role of homosexuality in his verse. Havelock Ellis is typical in this regard, brushing aside the homosexual sensibility as "negligible," and crying aloud that "Whitman represents for the first time since Christianity swept over the world, the reintegration, in a sane and whole hearted form, of the instincts of the entire man. . . ." In his own neo-Freudian terms, Ellis recapitulates the new-religious interpretation of Whitman as a beneficent anti-Christ. "Here is no thing of creeds and dogmas. Here is no stupefying list of 'Thou shalts' and 'Thou shalt nots' . . . To Whitman the Devil is dead, and the forces of good are slowly but surely working for the salvation of all." Reading for the "devil" God in any of the conventional senses of the word (He who says, "Thou shalt" and "Thou shalt not"), one sees the master-clue to the Whitman imago as the God of the Godless, the Father of the Fatherless, the Son of the Mother. The anti-Christian meaning of Whitman explains the odd united front that gathered about him, the "religious" Dr. Bucke and the "irreligious" Colonel Robert Ingersoll joined with the Nietzschean André Gide in his worship. Only D. H. Lawrence has ever challenged Whitman's claim to this honor, finding in him a final failure of nerve: "Then Whitman's mistake. The mistake of his interpretation of his watchword: Sympathy. . . . He still confounded it with Jesus' LOVE, and with Paul's CHARITY. Whitman, like all the rest of us, was at the end of the great emotional highway of Love. . . . The highway of Love ends at the

foot of the Cross. There is no beyond. . . . He needed to supersede
the Christian Charity, the Christian Love . . . in order to give his
Soul her last Freedom. . . . And he failed in so far as he failed to get
out of the old rut of Salvation." But one can hardly expect Lawrence
to be fair, since he coveted for himself the title of the anti-Christian
Christ.

To all other enemies of the superego as Church or State or pater-
familias, culture or Europe or "literature" Whitman has seemed a
sufficient idol, the bearded but motherly papa. In this sense, even his
homosexuality is necessary, not publicly proclaimed but "unconsciously" *there* for his disciples as for himself. It is as the Patriarch
who is not a father, and who has no Father on earth or in heaven, that
Whitman appeals to the Socialist, the advocate of the New Poetry, the
professional American, the undefined Democrat. Not realizing the
necessity to his myth of his impotence, his femininity, Whitman fell
into the error of inventing for himself six bastards when he was accused
of physically loving men; but it was a halfhearted addition to the legend,
imagined late and discounted even as it was told.

The true "sons" of Whitman are necessarily "spiritual," those leg-
endary readers who have never, of course, really read him, but who
correspond to the legendary poet: the mechanic, the bus driver, the
wounded soldier, bound to him by a love as pure as Dante's for Beatrice.
How careful he is in separating sex from sentiment (*Children of
Adam*), and sentiment from sex (the *Calamus* poems) — and how
American! Too American, perhaps, for us to see; it is only García
Lorca, a stranger in New York, who invokes this image precisely:

> Beautiful, Old Walt Whitman your beard full of butterflies . . .
> your thighs of a virginal Apollo . . . you moaned like a bird
> with its sex pierced with a needle . . .
> You dreaming of being a river and sleeping like a river
> with that comrade who would place in your breast
> a tiny pain of an ignorant leopard.

It is the heartbreaking innocence of this aspect of Whitman which
Lorca seizes, the unfallen tenderness of America behind the machine-
ridden cities; and he contrasts him sharply with the corrupted lovers
of the cities, whose meanings are quite different:

> queers of the cities, with your tumified flesh and your sullied
>   thought . . .
> harpies, assassins of doves
> slaves of women . . .

"Sleep, Walt," the Spanish poet concludes, finding in his virginal poet an odd promise of salvation, "and let a black boy announce to the golden whites the arrival of the reign of an ear of corn."

Not many worshipers of Walt, however, have been willing to accept him as the prophet of so ritual and mystic a revolution (surely the allusion to the Eleusinian mysteries that makes Walt the Ceres to the "black boy's" Kore is deliberate). From the beginning, he has been claimed as the forerunner of a more real, a more political "freedom," and as history has defined that ambiguous term more and more diversely, each faction, asserting its right to some meaning of the term, has held aloft its own image of Whitman. There has always been, to be sure, a suspicion that Whitman's "democracy" might be merely a rationalization of "adhesive" love; and in Germany, for instance, what began as a struggle between the "Uranians" and the Social Democrats over whether Whitman prophesied the coming of socialism or the emergence of the third sex ended in a rather vicious debunking of the "Yankee Saint" by the Uranian party.

But Socialists have always clung to Walt, raising his eidolon beside that of Karl Marx, while to others he has seemed linked to Mazzini and republicanism in general, as he is imagined in that most improbable of tributes by Swinburne (who later qualified his admiration drastically):

> Send but a song overseas for us,
>> Heart of their hearts who are free,
> Heart of their singer, to be for us
>> More than our singing can be;
> Ours, in the tempest at error
> With no light but the twilight of terror;
>> Send us a song oversea!

For the English poet, at first only uncertain as to whether he admired Whitman more as the apostle of freedom or of "the great god Man, which is God," Whitman stood for a specifically American experience. But in other European minds, both those that approved and those that were horrified, he was associated with an image of revolt that knew no national boundaries; and he was especially confused with those other serenely bearded rebels, Tolstoi and Hugo, in a way that reveals in the case of all three how different is their common mask from their stubbornly divergent selves. To the Continental who saw him as "the American" and America as somehow unitary, his image was blended with such improbable fellow countrymen as Theodore Roosevelt, the "professor of energy" (by Rubén Darío) or President Wilson (in post–World War I Germany, where it is said he was considered the real author of the Fourteen Points).

But strangest of Whitman's posthumous avatars was as a Marxist saint. While the French had been discovering in the author of *Leaves of Grass* a Nietzsche-like patron of intellectual anti-Christianity and an ancestor of *symbolisme,* the Germans had been finding behind the poem a figure that Johannes Becher was to name, finally, *Bruder Whitman,* Brother Whitman, Comrade Whitman; and they turned him willy-nilly into a dangerous poet, a revolutionary, whom the Central European police, convinced by the myth, felt obliged to ban just after the first World War. The *facts* matter not at all: that Whitman was a supporter of capitalism despite certain cagey reservations; that he despised trade-unions; that after his one long interview with a Socialist proselytizer, he murmured only, "What a beautiful young man!"—all this counted for certain sober critics and commentators, but not for the rank-and-file Marxists who knew only that Whitman represented the "Future" and so did they! In a sense, they were right, of course; for the legendary person he had created and released had taken on a life of its own and could make strange conversions long after the poet's death.

In Russia, too, an imaginary Whitman was drafted into the ranks of the revolutionaries, and by 1917 had become in the popular mind an unquestioned ancestral figure, so that *Leaves of Grass* was one of the first American books officially sponsored in translation by the Bolshevik government. But even before that, a poem by Whitman had been placed in the hands of the Soviet troops fighting the American Expeditionary Forces, as if to assure them that they, not the soldiers of the United States, were "America" as Whitman had defined it.

> Then courage European revolter, revoltress!
> For till all ceases neither must you cease.

"To a Foil'd European Revolutionaire" is, as poetry, Whitman at his worst—and the poetry inspired by "Comrade Whitman" does not rise above this example. Oddly enough, the redefined Communist Whitman was reimported into the United States, where along with translated Mayakovski, it became the official standard for "Proletarian Poetry" as practiced with fervor and imprecision in the darker 'thirties. The figure of Whitman that informed this kind of verse is classically invoked in a poem by Ben Maddow called "Red Decision," a brief citation from which must stand for all the rest:

Broad-hearted Whitman of the healthy beard
stiffen my infirm palate for this bread,
whose gritty leaven shall embowel me
to hold and nourish, with reasoning pity and force,
past fear and comfort or tranquillity,
in solemn hands, my tough majestic pen.

It is tempting and easy to mock efforts of this sort, which are, after all, no worse than Swinburne or most of the other poets destroyed by the image they chose to sponsor them. Whitman is an almost impossible muse, but it has taken us a long time to discover it. In recent years the Marxists have found themselves in almost uncontested possession of the figure of Whitman (challenged only by an occasional homespun versifier from the hills) as the practice and piety of our younger poets has shifted toward tradition and elegance; but for a while they stood in apparent solidarity with all that was "new" in American literature, with a whole horde of enthusiasts for whom Whitman was not only the whole future of poetry, but America itself.

The image of Whitman as the Bard, the popular voice, the very definition of the United States arises from a profound ambiguity in the poet himself; for one of the names he called his Fancy, his Mask was "America." "I hear America singing . . . I celebrate myself and sing myself . . ." The image of Walt swells and is extended until it merges indistinguishably with the body of an imaginary continent, and the continent with the vision of comradeship, with "Democracy *ma femme.*" In the end, there are two wives of Whitman and the two are one: himself and his country: Walt Whitman *ma femme* and America *ma femme.* The French is not merely accidental and comical; it gives away the whole game.

Walt Whitman's America was made in France, the Romantic notion out of Rousseau and Chateaubriand of an absolute anti-Europe, an utter anticulture made flesh, the Noble Savage as a Continent. And from the same sources, Whitman derived the ideal of a national poetry, the belief that a country did not really exist until a poet discovered it for the imagination. The irony of such literary ideas is that they must pretend to be unliterary, antiliterary, the expression of a purely native and ingenuous humanism.

Come, Muse, migrate from Greece and Ionia,
Cross out please those immensely overpaid accounts . . .

But no European is long fooled by the pose of barbarity that Europe invented; Thomas Mann, for instance, who loved Whitman, identified his meaning with the *humanitas* of Novalis—and with the thought of Goethe himself!

We have come to understand that the only American writers who can transcend the European tradition are those who begin frankly from it; that the "pure" Americans endure becoming unconsciously stereotypes devised by Europeans weary of the burden of their culture. The unreality of Whitman's America—that is, of the European dream of America—is revealed in its need to be forever moved toward a vanishing horizon, to be defined as the Absolute West. It is never the known and experienced world, but always the dreamed one over the next ridge, beyond the next river: the world of a legendary innocence, of Experience as Innocence, where one can undergo all and remain virgin. It is for this reason that Whitman the New Yorker was redreamed (in part by himself) as the poet of a "West" which he had not even visited when *Leaves of Grass* took shape. It is utterly misleading to remember Whitman as a Populist, plein-air poet; for at his best he is a singer of urban life, like Baudelaire, dedicated to redeeming for the imagination the world of industry, the life of cities. It is not to field or farmland that he invites the Muse, but to the urban kitchen with its window opening on the view of factories:

> By thud of machinery and shrill steam-whistle undismay'd,
> Bluff'd not a bit by drain-pipe, gasometers, artificial fertilizers;
> Smiling and pleas'd with palpable intent to stay,
> She's here, install'd amid the kitchen-ware.

But this is a witty Whitman and a precise observer who jibes ill with the figure of the diffuse and humorless Tribal Bard that the all-American Whitmanites have tried to create. *Their* Whitman has been classically defined by Edgar Lee Masters. "It is not because Whitman is a better poet than Emerson that he may be called the father of American poetry. . . . It is because Whitman wrote for the American tribe and the American idea. . . . Whitman was the tribal prophet and poet. . . . Whitman had the right idea, namely, that poetry, the real written word, must come out of the earth. . . . It is no wonder that a man as sincere as Whitman, whose sincerity chose prosody without rhyme, meter or ornament, had to endure the sneers and chatter of New York critics . . . who often miss the important, the real and truly American art."

But, one wants to protest, all these ideas come precisely out of "books and erudition"—and it is no use pleading in self-defense that they are bad books and spotty erudition: the fear of New Yorkers (critics or Wall Street bankers, it scarcely matters), provinciality as true virtue, "sincerity" as the sole aesthetic criterion, the notion that rhyme and meter are somehow meretricious, the adulation of the "tribe." What good to point out that these are the dreams of the effete at their most exhausted, the last nostalgia of the hyperaesthete for a mythic "natural." Such ideas die hard because they appeal to those haters of literature unprepared to appear under their true colors; "emancipated" puritans and social reformers, superpatriots and Communists who fear and distrust art but like to boast that some of their best friends are poets! When challenged to name one, they can always evoke Walt Whitman. Poor Walt! It is the final indignity: to have become the image of the antiartist, of the poet as despiser of poetry, of America as an anticulture.

It gets harder and harder to remember that once (only two wars ago!) his name was the rallying cry of the literary avant-garde; New Sex, New Society and New Poetry, they seemed three persons of a single god, and Whitman was its prophet. *Poetry,* the magazine founded by Harriet Monroe, still carries a tag from Whitman; and in its pioneer days it evoked as a syndrome, anticonventional and antibourgeois, T. S. Eliot, Pound, Whitman, Amy Lowell, imagism, free verse, Sandburg, Frost, and E. A. Robinson. Then and for a long time afterward, other little magazines were sponsoring with equal fervor new directions in social organization and in experimental verse. To this blur of enthusiasm the prophetic blur at the heart of the Whitman image corresponded exactly; he is the presiding genius of an alliance based on the single slogan: "Make It New!"

It was an alliance that could not survive its first victories; quite soon the Socialist new poet was regarding the converted Catholic novelist with hostility; the rediscoverer of metaphysical wit and classical form was watching warily the exponent of uncorseted dithyrambs; the advocate of escape from emotion was wondering how he had ever enlisted beside the enthusiasts of phallic consciousness. In an introduction to the *Selected Poems* of Ezra Pound, Eliot has put his own protest on record: "I did not read Whitman until much later in life, and had to conquer an aversion to his form, as well as much of his matter, in order to do so. I am equally certain—it is indeed obvious—that Pound owes nothing to Whitman. This is an elementary observation. . . ." Amy Lowell had already detached herself with a haughty statement. "Often and often I read in the daily, weekly and monthly press, that modern vers libre writers derive their form from Walt Whitman. As a matter of fact, most of them got it from French Symbolist poets. . . ." It is toward Walt's Communist kidnapers that she is glancing, for she adds, "The last ignominy to him would be the usage of his words to tear down the governmental structure that he loved." And she has concluded with the coolest of snubs: "It is perhaps sadly significant that the three modern poets who most loudly acknowledge his leadership are all of recent foreign extraction. . . ."

This is the beginning of an attack that does not end until Whitman is transformed from a figure symbolizing the way poetry must go to a half-comic image personifying the wrong turning, the temptation to formlessness and disorder, the blind alley of the pseudo poet. Pound's offer of a negotiated peace finds no supporters even among his own followers:

> I make a pact with you, Walt Whitman—
> I have detested you long enough.
> I come to you as a grown child
> Who has had a pig-headed father;
> I am old enough to make friends . . .

This is an entirely new resistance to *Leaves of Grass,* not the protest of the anti-Jacobin and the genteel, the demurrer of a James Russell Lowell or a Holmes, feeling the hungry generations treading him down; not the horrified "scientific" rejection of a Nordau or Lombroso, classifying Whitman as insane, but the refusal of a poet by the very future on which he had staked all. It is the liveliest minds that begin to turn away from him, not only the reactionary wits like Wyndham Lewis: "Walt Whitman was, I feel sure, the father of the American Baby. . . . Walt showed all those enthusiastic habits we associate with the Baby. He rolled about naked in the Atlantic surf, uttering 'barbaric yawps' . . . he was prone to 'cosmic raptures.' . . . He was a great big heavy old youngster of the perfect Freudian type, with the worst kind of enthusiasm in the Greek sense of the word." To begin with, it is against the Mask of Whitman that they revolt, for they do not want the Son of the Mother for *their* Father; they are after new ancestors, a tradition not of the traditionless but of the traditional. But they find it hard to believe that there is a genuine poet behind the distasteful persona. Only in Europe does Whitman continue to belong to the young, to the creating writers; in the United States he becomes the possession of those new philistines who love the renewal of the day before yesterday —and of the more liberal-minded scholars.

It is these scholars who have been in recent years creating a legend of Whitman's fame, a rags-to-riches story of a slow, but unbroken triumph over the reservations of the shortsighted genteel; and in the interests of this legend they have failed to record (perhaps they have not even noticed) the decline of their poet's reputation among our best practicing poets. Yet the *essential* fact about Whitman as a force in American poetry is precisely what Gay Wilson Allen, for instance, does not even hint at in his *Handbook*, that for the last twenty-five years Whitman has been a chief whipping boy of many of our best poets and critics.

The defeat of Whitman as the informing image of the Poet, as our bearded Muse of the New, is ironically sealed by an attempted celebration in Hart Crane's *The Bridge* of his figure as the Meistersinger of America.

> *Panis Angelicus*! Eyes tranquil with the blaze
> Of love's own diametric gaze, of love's amaze . . .
> Our Meistersinger, thou set breath in steel;
> And it was thou who on the boldest heel
> Stood up and flung the span on even wing
> Of that great Bridge, our Myth, whereof I sing!
>
> . . . .
>
> My hand
>   in yours,
>   Walt Whitman—
>
>   so—

This is hardly Crane at his best. Even the characteristic incoherence is a faked, a second-rate incoherence—not a blending at incandescent temperature but an ersatz fusion; and the attack on the failures of Crane's poem which followed its publication centered on this passage and on the image behind it. The *locus classicus* is the review by Yvor Winters that appeared in *Poetry* for June 1930, asserting that *The Bridge* at its best "carries the epic quality of the Whitmanian vision (the vision of humanity *en masse* or undifferentiated) to the greatest dignity and power of which it is, probably, capable . . ." thus proving under the most favorable conditions "the impossibility of getting anywhere with the Whitmanian inspiration. No writer of comparable ability has struggled with it before, and, with Mr. Crane's wreckage in view, it seems highly unlikely that any writer of comparable genius will struggle with it again."

Doubtless, one of the troubles with the "Cape Hatteras" section of

Crane's poem is the falsification by Crane (probably even to himself) of his relation to the image of Whitman. The homosexual sensibility which they shared is ignored in favor of Whitman's legendary representativeness as an "American"; besides, Crane, attracted with one part of his mind to Eliot, is already ridden with doubts about Whitman's true worth. A letter to Allen Tate reveals his ambivalence. "It's true that my rhapsodic address to him [Whitman] in the Bridge exceeds any exact evaluation of the man. . . . There isn't much use in my tabulating the qualified, yet persistent, reasons I have for my admiration of him. . . . You've heard me roar at too many of his lines to doubt that I can spot his worst, I'm sure. . . ." The myth and the poet had begun to come apart for Crane; and I suspect they cannot be put together by an act of will. Certainly, one has the impression that "Cape Hatteras" is not believed in but *worked up.*

Whatever the truth about these matters, the failure of *The Bridge* was interpreted not as Crane's failure, but as Whitman's. Tate, Blackmur, and others seconded Winters, and this judgment of the Whitmanian imago via *The Bridge* soon became a standard conviction of the "New Critics," indeed, one of the few beliefs which actually are shared by that ill-assorted congeries. In Blackmur a typical contrast is added to complete the position: "Baudelaire aimed at control, Whitman at release. It is for these reasons that the influence of Whitman was an impediment to the *practise* (to be distinguished from the reading) of poetry, and that the influence of Baudelaire is re-animation itself. . . ."

What began as an "advanced" minority opinion has tended to become at least an important orthodoxy, if not *the* orthodoxy of the young, changing emphasis along the way so that Whitman is regarded not only as a bad "influence" but even as a bad poet, the founder of an inferior tradition. William Van O'Connor sums up the position in his recent study, *Sense and Sensibility in Modern Poetry.* "But Whitman and his followers—like Robinson Jeffers, Vachel Lindsay, Edgar Lee Masters, Carl Sandburg, Stephen Vincent Benét and William Rose Benét, and later Paul Engle, August Derleth, Muriel Rukeyser, Ben Maddow, and Alfred Hayes . . . are not in the line of American writers who have deepened our knowledge of human motivation or action. They are, in so far as they are followers of Whitman, away from the tradition which runs from Hawthorne and Melville through James and Eliot."

Though such amalgams as this seem to me to exploit shamelessly the device of "guilt by association," I sympathize with Mr. O'Connor's effort to isolate the exploiters of what he calls "the historico-mythic equivalent of America." I, too, am repelled by those who do not make poems but manipulate a prefabricated theme and feel that by naming an undefined essence "America" they can turn it into a universal touch-stone. I do not even object to setting the "Whitmanians" against what-ever equivalent of the metaphysical-symbolist tradition can be found in our literature, except as such a contrast implies that one tradition guarantees, or another makes impossible, poetry. Whitman, at least, succeeds, whatever his assumptions, in being a poet more often than it is ever possible to remember; he is not *merely* his myth, either as he himself expresses it or as it persists in this line of spiritual descent.

I know why Mr. O'Connor and many others find it hard to admit Whitman's excellence; one does not easily come to love a poet who is used as a weapon against oneself and one's favorite writers. And Whitman has become precisely such a weapon in the hands of those who (Van Wyck Brooks is an example) condemn Eliot or Pound on the grounds that they have rejected all that Whitman affirms. It is vain to retort with the commonplace that "poetry affirmeth nought," for Whitman has taught us otherwise. Besides, it is turn and turn about; once the sides were chosen up—Baudelaire against Whitman; Poe, Melville, or Hawthorne against Whitman; Eliot against Whitman— warfare was inevitable. You cannot beat Whitman over the head with Eliot and be surprised when the process is reversed. Such conflicts have a certain strategic value so long as we remember that the causes for which they are fought are not really the poets who bear the same names, but merely their images, tricked out to horrify or allure. Whit-man is no more devil than messiah. He is a poet whom we must begin now to rescue from parody as well as apotheosis.

We shall not return to the same Whitman from which we started; twenty-five years of dissent cannot be undone. It is to our *own* Whit-man that we come back, and we come by our own roads, via authors whom Whitman would perhaps have despised. It is not from his friends that we ask letters of recommendation but from those who had no reason to love him, from Henry James, for instance, or from Gerard Manley Hopkins. Even Randall Jarrell has felt obliged to remind us (albeit ironically) in a recent admirable essay, that James was moved almost to tears in reading Whitman to Edith Wharton, and that Hop-kins wrote to Bridges, "I always knew in my heart Walt Whitman's mind to be more like my own than any other man's living. . . ." One laughs a little remembering Yeats's account of how he scarcely listened to Hopkins, whom he met in his father's studio, because he was carrying in his own pocket *Leaves of Grass*; but one laughs wryly, for it is the joke of history which is always on *us*!

It is not to the life-affirmer we are returning, but to the elegiac Whitman, the poet of death. "Merging! And Death!" D. H. Lawrence wrote accusingly of Whitman. "The great merge into the womb. Woman. And after that, the merging of comrades: man-for-man love. . . . Woman is inadequate for the last merging. So the next step is the merging of man-for-man love. And this is on the brink of death. It slides over into death." But the case for the prosecution has become the case for the defense: another joke of history! Dismayed by an optimism in which we no longer believe, a self-assurance that seems to us obscene, we find with relief in *Leaves of Grass* that "blackness ten times black" which Melville once thrilled to discover in Hawthorne. We are pleased to find surviving the hearty eidolon, the melancholy poet who began writing stories about the poor boy flogged to death by a wicked teacher, to honor "the dusky demon and brother" whom Walt did not forget. It is his attackers who have defined for us the Whitman we can love; even such negative and furious onslaughts as those of Esther Shephard and Harvey O'Higgins have succeeded in destroying not the poet but the legend which obscured him.

How different the meaning of what such critics have found is for us than it was for them! Discovering among Whitman's papers the cardboard butterfly with which he faked the famous portrait; learning that the untainted American family of which he liked to boast was ridden with madness and disease; finding a host of proofs that the New Orleans love affair, the vaunted bastards were deliberate hoaxes— his debunkers were ready to write off Walt as "insincere." To them this seemed to destroy his validity as a poet-prophet, to reveal him as "only" a self-advertiser, a poseur, not original or a Democrat or even a lusty breeder. But those of us who know that poetry (God forbid that we should attempt to judge the *man*!) is precisely a matter of cardboard butterflies on real fingers, that the wit and tension of a poem depend on the distance between the given and the imagined, are grateful to Miss Shephard and Mr. O'Higgins for having rescued Walt Whitman from "life" (i.e., the clichés of politics and pseudo mysticism) and having restored him to art.

Our Walt Whitman is the slyest of artificers, the artificer of "sincerity," and if this sounds like a joke, there is no reason why even the greatest poetry cannot be a joke on someone, not excluding its author. It does not seem enough to me to say, as G. W. Stonier has in one of the more perceptive comments on Whitman, "His duplicity staggers.

He was a fine poet and a charlatan," because this implies that his fine poetry is based on something other than his charlatanism. Whitman's trickery is essential, not accidental, to his poems. Like the mannerists, like Shakespeare, who is the greatest among them, he is a player with illusion; his center is a pun on the self; his poetry is a continual shimmering on the surfaces of concealment and revelation that is at once pathetic and comical.

His duplicity is, I feel, a peculiarly American duplicity, that doubleness of our self-consciousness, which our enemies too easily call hypocrisy, but which arises from our belief that what we dream rather than what we are is our essential truth. The Booster and the Pharisee are the standard caricatures of the American double man, and Whitman was both Booster and Pharisee. Condemned to play the Lusty Innocent, the Noble Savage, by a literary tradition that had invented his country before he inhabited it, Whitman had no defenses. The whole Western world demanded of him the lie in which we have been catching him out, the image of America in which we no longer believe; the whole world cried to him, "Be the Bard we can only dream! Chant the freedom we have imagined as if it were real!"

But he was not "America"; he was only a man, ridden by impotence and anxiety, by desire and guilt, furtive and stubborn and half-educated. That he became the world's looked-for, ridiculous darling is astonishing enough; that he remained a poet through it all is scarcely credible. He has survived his images, and at last the outlived posturing, the absurd ideas, the rhetoric borrowed and misunderstood fall away, until only the poetry remains, and the poet, anonymous in the end as they were in the beginning.

I and this mystery here we stand.

KENNETH BURKE

Policy Made Personal
Whitman's Verse and Prose-Salient Traits

THE PLAN here is to consider first Whitman's statement of policy in *Democratic Vistas*. Even there his views of history, society, and nature are personalized somewhat. But the full job of personalization is done in his *Leaves of Grass*, which is to be considered in a second section. And finally, since both of these sections are general in their approach, a third section will put the main stress upon one poem, "When Lilacs Last in the Dooryard Bloom'd." Throughout, however, we shall proceed as much as practicable by the inspection and comparison of contexts. Unless otherwise specified, all words or expressions in quotation marks are Whitman's. (Perhaps a better subtitle would be: On Interrelations Among Key Terms in Whitman's Language.)

I. VISTAS

The design of Whitman's essentially idealistic thought is neatly indicated in the three stages of historical unfolding he assigns to "America, type of progress." This alignment seems a handy place to spin from.

The first stage was embodied in the Declaration of Independence, the Constitution, and its Amendments. It "was the planning and putting on record the political foundation rights of immense masses of people . . . not for classes, but for universal man."

The second stage is in the "material prosperity" that resulted after the democratic foundations had been laid: "wealth, labor-saving machines . . . a currency," etc.

A third stage, still to come but "arising out of the previous ones," would bring about the corresponding "spiritualization" of the nation's sheerly material development.

The first and third stages are in the realm of idea, or spirit. The second stage is in the realm of matter. Writing his essay a few years after the close of the Civil War, he placed himself and his times in stage two, a time marked by "hollowness at heart," lack of honest belief in "the underlying principles of the States," "depravity of the business classes," while all politics were "saturated in corruption" except the judiciary ("and the judiciary is tainted"). "A mob of fashionably dressed speculators and vulgarians . . . crude defective streaks in all the strata of the common people . . . the alarming spectacle of parties usurping the government . . . these savage, wolfish parties* . . . delicatesse . . . polite conformity . . . exterior appearance and show, mental and other, built entirely on the idea of caste" . . . in sum: "Pride, competition, segregation, vicious wilfulness, and license beyond example, brood already upon us."

One could cite many other statements of like attitude. But the idealistic design of his thinking permitted him without discouragement to take full note of such contemporary ills, and perhaps even to intensify them as one step in his essay. For against the dissatisfactions of the present, he could set his "planned Idea," a promise for the future. Since "the fruition of democracy, on aught like a grand scale, resides altogether in the future," he would "presume to write, as it were, upon things that exist not, and travel by maps yet unmade, and a blank." Thus, the technically negative nature of the "fervid and tremendous Idea" is made in effect positive, so far as *personal* considerations go. By seeing contemporary conditions in terms of future possibilities, in "vistas" that stressed "results to come," he could treat "America and democracy as convertible terms," while having high hopes for both. He says, "It is useless to deny" that "Democracy grows rankly up the thickest, noxious, deadliest plants and fruits of all—brings worse and worse invaders—needs newer, larger, stronger, keener compensations and compellers"; but, in line with post-Hegelian promises, he saw in any greater challenge the possibility of a correspondingly greater response.

In sum, then, as regards the basic design of his thinking, the *Vistas* found elation in a project for the "spiritualization of our nation's wealth." (He likes words like "richness" and "luxuriance," words that readily suggest both material and spiritual connotations, gaining resonance and persuasiveness from this ambiguity.) "The extreme

---

* Since political parties are themselves a point at which present organization and future promises meet, we might expect him to waver here, and he does. Thus: "I advise you to enter more strongly yet into politics"—but also "Disengage yourself from parties." The wavering even invades his syntax, when he says that he knows "nothing grander, better exercise, better digestion, more positive proof of the past, the triumphant result of faith in human kind, than a well-contested American national election."

business energy, and this almost maniacal appetite for wealth prevalent in the United States, are parts of amelioration and progress," he says (in terms that, of all things, suggest Marxist patterns of thought with regard to material development under capitalism) ; but a different order of motives is manifest in the statement (he would probably have said "promulgation") of his ideal: "Offsetting the material civilization of our race . . . must be its moral civilization."

If, by very definition, one can view all materially acquisitive behavior in terms of ideal future fulfillment, it follows that the poet could contemplate with "joy" the industrious industrial conquest of the continent. Not until late in life (after his paralytic stroke) does this "ecstatic" champion of the "athletic" and "electric" body turn from identification with the feller of trees (as in *Song of the Broad-Axe*) to identification with the fallen tree itself (as in *Song of the Redwood-Tree*), though he always had fervid ways of being sympathetic to child, adult, and the elderly. Our point is simply that the zestfulness of the typical Whitman survey could follow logically from his promissory principle, his idealization of the present in terms of the future.

Halfway between the realm of materials amassed by his countrymen's "oceanic, variegated, intense, practical energy" and the realm of spirit, or idea, we might place his cult of the sturdy human body, its "spinal," "athletic," "magnetic" qualities and the "appetites" that make for "sensuous luxuriance." (As the recipe also called for a male type "somewhat flushed," we dare wonder ironically whether his notion of the perfect "manly" temperament also concealed a syndrome of symptoms, an idealistic recognition, without realistic diagnosis, of the hypertension that must have preceded his paralysis. Surely, prophesying after the event, we might propose that Whitman's headlong style should involve high blood pressure as its nosological counterpart.)

For an "over-arching" term here, Whitman could speak of "nature" in ways that, while clearly referring to the materialistic on one side, also have pontificating aspects leading into a Beyond, along Emersonian lines. (In fact, toward the close of the *Vistas*, one is often strongly reminded of Emerson's earlier and longer transcendentalist essay, *Nature*, first published in 1836.) Democracy was Nature's "younger brother," and Science was "twin, in its field, of Democracy in its." But such equations were idealistically weighted to one side: for while "Dominion strong is the body's ; dominion stronger is the mind's."

Somewhere between the grounding of his position in time, and its grounding in eternity, there is its grounding in terms of personality (two of his special words to this end being "identity" and "nativity").

For grounding in time, one obvious resource is a contrast with some previous time (antithesis being one of the three major stylistic resources, as we are informed in Aristotle's *Rhetoric*). But though "democracy" is thus pitted against "feudalism," Whitman admonishes that "feudalism, caste, ecclesiastical traditions . . . still hold essentially, by their spirit, even in this country, entire possession of the more important fields." For "All smells of princes' favors." And "The United States are destined either to surmount the gorgeous history of feudalism, or else prove the most tremendous failure of time." Whereas now we tend to think of Shakespeare as poignantly at the crossing between the feudal and the modern, the antithetical genius of Whitman's scheme led him to say: "The great poems, Shakespeare included, are poisonous to the idea of the pride and dignity of the common people." For though Shakespeare was conceded to be "rich," and "luxuriant as the sun," he was the "artist and singer of feudalism in its sunset." In contrast, Whitman called: "Come forth, sweet democratic despots of the west." And being against "parlors, parasols, piano-songs," he matched his praise of the "divine average" by words against "the mean flat average." Declaring, "We stand, live, move, in the huge flow of our age's materialism," he quickly added, "in its spirituality." And "to offset chivalry," he would seek "a knightlier and more sacred cause today." In so far as the claims of traditional culture were effete and pretentious (and "for a single class alone"), he admonished against "Culture"—and later, apologists of Nazism could take over the tenor of his slogans by the simple device of but half-hearing him.

As for eternity: His attacks upon traditional ecclesiastical forms were stated in terms of an "all penetrating Religiousness" that vigorously proclaimed its scorn of "infidels." He always identified democracy with what he called "the religious element," however that might differ from the norms of conventional churchgoing (and it differed greatly, as regards its relation to his cult of the "body electric").

His notion of "succession" (a eulogistic word that sounds nearly like his very dyslogistic one, "secession") we have already touched upon. It is in line with the typical nineteenth-century doctrine of permanent evolution, into ever higher forms, a design that falls in the realm of time, so far as the manifestations of history are concerned, but that would be above time, in so far as its operation were constant. "The law over all, the law of laws, is the law of successions; that of the superior law, in time, gradually supplanting and overwhelming the inferior one." Fittingly, the essay reverts to this "law" in the paragraph-long closing sentence, where America, "illumined and illuming," is saluted in terms of the ideal future, when she will have "become a full-formed world, and divine Mother, not only of material but spiritual worlds, in ceaseless succession, through time—the main thing being the average, the bodily, the concrete, the democratic, the popular, on which all the superstructures of the future are to permanently rest."

The lines succinctly assemble the main components of his Ideal Matrix, or "divine Mother." (And what better words for an *ending* than "permanently rest"?) But the personalizing of this "Mother" (the democratic creed) will take on attributes not strictly germane to either the politics of democracy or the personality of motherhood.

The logic of his terminology centers in his emphasis upon the individual person ("rich, luxuriant, varied personalism"). In proclaiming that "the ripeness of religion" is to be sought in the "field of individuality," and is "a result that no organization or church can ever achieve," he automatically sets up the dialectical conditions for a principle of division matched by a principle of merger. While his brand of "personalism" will "promulge" the "precious idiocrasy and special nativity and intention that he is, the man's self," all such individual selves are to be joined in democratic union, or "cohesion"; and the result is "ensemble-Individuality," an "idiocrasy of universalism," since the "liberalist of today" seeks "not only to individualize, but to universalize." And while the aim is to formulate "one broad, primary, universal, common platform," he says, "even for the treatment of the universal" it is good "to reduce the whole matter to the consideration of a single self, a man, a woman, on permanent grounds."

In sum: There is "the All, and the idea of All, with the accompanying idea of eternity" (the poems will speak of "the all-mother," and the "Mother of All"). And in silence, in the "solitariness of individuality," one can "enter the pure ether of veneration," to "commune" with the "mysteries" and the "unutterable." Or (as regards the timely), "individuality" and its "unimpeded branchings" will "flourish best under imperial republican forms" (for the grandeur of spiritualized democratic "expansion" will make for an "empire of empires").*

So we have the "idea of perfect individualism," of "completeness in separation," with its dialectical counterpart: "the identity of the Union at all hazards." Not only must man become "a law, a series of

---

* "It seems as if the Almighty had spread before this nation charts of imperial destinies, dazzling as the sun yet with many a deep intestine difficulty, and human aggregate of cantankerous imperfection—saying, lo! the roads, the only plans of development, long and varied with all terrible balks and ebullitions." Might not these lines serve well as motto for his *Song of the Open Road*, and as indicating a notable ingredient in his cult of the roadway generally?

laws, unto himself"; also "the great word Solidarity has arisen." The "individualism, which isolates" is but "half only," and has for its other half the "adhesiveness or love, that fuses." Thus, both of these trends (contradictory or complementary?) are "vitalized by religion," for you in your solitude can "merge yourself" in the "divine." (A sheerly politico-economic variant of this dialectic for fitting the one and the many together is in his statement: "The true gravitation-hold of liberalism in the United States will be a more universal ownership of property, general homesteads, general comfort—a vast, inter-twining reticulation of wealth.")

But if the three stages are handiest as a way into the underlying idealistic *design* of Whitman's thinking, perhaps the most succinct *doctrinal* passage is this:

"Long ere the second centennial arrives, there will be some forty to fifty States, among them Canada and Cuba. When the present century closes, our population will be sixty or seventy millions. The Pacific will be ours, and the Atlantic mainly ours. There will be daily electric communication with every part of the globe. What an age! What a land! Where, elsewhere, one so great? The individuality of one nation must then, as always, lead the world. Can there be any doubt who the leader ought to be? Bear in mind, though, that nothing less than the mightiest original non-subordinated SOUL has ever really, gloriously led, or ever can lead."

Then comes the very important addition, in parentheses: "This SOUL—its other name, in these Vistas, is LITERATURE." Then follows typical talk of "ideals," and of a "richness" and "vigor" that will be in letters "luxuriantly."

The essay's opening reference to "lessons" attains its fulfillment in these views of Whitman on the didactic or moralizing element in his ideal literature, its social service in the training of personalities. By the "mind," which builds "haughtily," the national literature shall be endowed "with grand and archetypal models," as we confront the "momentous spaces" with a "new and greater personalism," aided by the "image-making faculty."

Here, then, is the grand mélange: "Arrived now, definitely, at an apex for these Vistas," Whitman sees in dream "a new and greater literatus order," its members "always one, compact in soul," though "separated . . . by different dates or States." This band would welcome materialistic trends both "for their oceanic practical grandeur" and "for purposes of spiritualization." And by "serving art in its highest," such a "band of brave and true" would also be "serving God, and serving humanity."

Such a literature would affirm the "fervid comradeship," "adhesive love," between man and man that Whitman so strongly associated with his evangel of democracy. And as for woman, the "prophetic literature of these States," inspired by "Idealism," will train toward "the active redemption of woman," and "a race of perfect Mothers."

He offers four portraits of ideal female types: a servant, a business-woman, a housewife, and a fourth that we might call a grand old lady ("a resplendent person . . . known by the name of the Peacemaker"). It is particularly relevant to look more closely at this fourth figure.

Whitman has just been referring to "that indescribable perfume of genuine womanhood . . . which belongs of right to all the sex, and is, or ought to be, the invariable atmosphere and common aureola of old as well as young." The next paragraph begins: "My dear mother once described to me . . . ," etc. Eighty years old, this fourth type of personality that his mother is said to have described was a kind of grandmotherly Whitman. She had lived "down on Long Island." She was called the "Peacemaker" because of her role as "the reconciler in the land." She was "of happy and sunny temperament," was "very neighborly"; and she "possessed a native dignity." "She was a sight to look upon, with her large figure, her profuse snow-white hair (un-coifed by any head-dress or cap) . . . and peculiar personal mag-netism"—and when reading the word on which the recital of his four "portraits" ends, might we not fittingly recall that Whitman's poems are dotted with references to the "electric" and "magnetic"?

We consider this all of a piece: the steps from "the indescribable perfume of genuine womanhood," to "My dear mother," to the grand-motherly figure in which this entire set of portraits culminates (and thus toward which the series might be said to have tended from the start). Frankly, we stress the point for use later, when we shall be considering the scent of lilacs, "the perfume strong I love," mentioned in commemoration of the poet's great dead democratic hero. Mean-while, a few more considerations should be noted, before we turn from his prose statement of policy to its personalizing in his verse.

We should recall his principle of cultural *ascesis* (the notion that "political democracy" is "life's gymnasium . . . fit for freedom's ath-letes," and that books are "in highest sense, an exercise, a gymnast's struggle"). It is easy to see how thought thus of a *studious athleticism* might, on the one hand, proclaim "health, pride, acuteness, noble as-pirations" as the "motive-elements of the grandest style"; on the other hand, given the "appetites" that go with such exercisings and exertions, the poet might find no embarrassments in equating democracy with the grandeur of ever expanding empire.

But there is one mild puzzler to be noted with regard to the Whitman cult of democratic expansionism. When saying that the "spine-character of the States will probably run along the Ohio, Missouri and Mississippi rivers, and west and north of them, including Canada," he describes the "giant growth" thus: "From the north, intellect, the sun of things, also the idea of unswayable justice, anchor amid the last, the wildest tempests. From the south the living soul, the animus of good and bad, haughtily admitting no demonstration but its own. While from the west itself comes solid personality, with blood and brawn, and the deep quality of all-accepting fusion."

One automatically waits for some mention of the east here—but there is none. Interestingly enough, one of the poems ("To the Leaven'd Soil They Trod") discusses "vistas" and *ends* on a similar design:

The prairie draws me close, as the father to bosom broad the son,
The Northern ice and rain that began me nourish me to the end,
But the hot sun of the South is to fully ripen my songs.

Presumably, the poet mentions only three points of the compass, since he was born in the *East*, and was so *tendency-minded*. And perhaps, since the *Vistas* contain the equation, "the democratic, the west," the East is, by the dialectical or rhetorical pressures of antithesis, the vestigially and effetely "feudal," except in so far as it is inspirited by the other three sources of motivation. (South, by the way, is in Whitman's idiom the place from which "perfume" comes. As regards North, we must admit to not having fully done our lessons at this time.)

A few further points, before turning from the *Vistas* to the *Leaves*:

In connection with the notion of guidance through literature, Whitman writes: "A strong mastership of the general inferior self by the superior self, is to be aided, secured, indirectly, but surely, by the literatus." And we might remember this word "mastership," to puzzle over it, when in the poem of the "Lilacs" he says: "Yet the lilac with mastering odor holds me," even though we may not quite succeed in fitting the passages to each other.

And we should note Whitman's words in praise of a strong political digestion, since they bear so directly upon the relation between his design and his doctrine: "And as, by virtue of its cosmical, antiseptic power, Nature's stomach is fully strong enough not only to digest the morbific matter always presented . . . but even to change such contributions into nutriment for highest use and life—so American democracy's."

Such faith in the virtues of a healthy appetite is doubtless implied when, on the subject of political corruption, Whitman assures us that "the average man . . . remains immortal owner and boss, deriving good uses, somehow, out of any sort of servant in office." (Or, more generally, here is the encouragement of the sprout-out-of-rot principle.) At every step along the way, whatever tax is levied by their Lordships, Favoritism and Dishonesty, it remains a fact that Democracy does build its roads and schools and courthouses—and the catalogue of its accumulations, when listed under one national head, becomes truly "oceanic" and "over-arching." But at the mention of catalogues, we might well turn to a survey of the verse.

II. LEAVES

No two opening lines of a poet's work ever indicated more clearly the sheer dialectics of a position than in the "Inscription" with which *Leaves of Grass* begins:

> One's-Self I sing, a simple separate person,
> Yet utter the word Democratic, the word En-Masse.

For a poet generally so voluble, this entire poem of eight lines is astoundingly efficient. Note how the second stanza (proclaiming that "physiology" is equally important with "physiognomy" and "brain," and that he sings "The Female equally with the Male") ambiguously translates his code into its corresponding *sexual* terms. Then, in the third stanza, he merges life, work, God's laws, song, and his futuristic cult of the present, all under the sign of strong motives and hopeful attitudes:

> Of Life immense in passion, pulse, and power,
> Cheerful, for freest action form'd under the laws divine,
> The Modern Man I sing.

The main themes that are lacking are: (1) his merging of birth and death in the allness of the mother, and (2) his stress upon perpetual passage (what would Whitman do without the word "pass" or its components: "I come and I depart"?). And, of course, the notable equating of democracy with the love of male for male is manifest here only if we read as a *double-entendre* his words about Male and Female (though most likely they were not so intended).

In his "oceanic" accumulation of details, the catalogues that characterize most of his longer poems (such as *Salut au Monde!*), there is obviously the "spiritualization" of matter. Here is his primary resource for those loosely yet thematically guided associations of ideas which enable him to "chant the chant of dilation or pride." Of such spiritual possessions, he has "stores and plenty to spare." Who was more qualified than Whitman to write a *Song of the Exposition* with its closing apostrophe to the "universal Muse" and maternal Union: "While we rehearse our measureless wealth, it is for thee, dear Mother"? In effect, the Whitman catalogue locates the rhetorical device of amplification in the very nature of things.

It is possible that, after long inspection, we might find some "overarching" principle of development that "underlies" his typical lists. Always, of course, they can be found to embody some principle of repetitive form, some principle of classification whereby the various items fall under the same head (as with the third stanza of the *Salut*, for instance, which races through a scattering of nationalities, with a scattering of details hastily allotted to each: the Australians "pursuing the wild horse," the Spanish semipleonastically dancing "with castanets in the chestnut shade," "echoes from the Thames," "fierce French liberty songs," and so on, ending with the Hindoo "teaching his favorite pupil the loves, wars, adages, transmitted safely from poets who wrote three thousand years ago"). Some critic might also discern a regular canon of *development* in such "turbulent" heapings. Meanwhile, in any case, there are the many variations by internal contrast (as with varying rhythm and length of line, or as the variations on "out of" that mark the opening lines of "Out of the Cradle Endlessly Rocking": out of, over, down from, up from, out from, from the, from your, from under, from those, from such, borne hither). And even where epanaphora is extreme, there are large tidal changes from stanza to stanza, or rhetorical forms that suggest the shifting of troops in military maneuvers.

"Melange mine own . . . Omnes! Omnes! . . . the word En-Masse . . . the One formed out of all . . . toward all . . . made ONE IDENTITY . . . they shall flow and unite . . . merge and unite . . . to merge all in the travel they tend to . . . All, all, toward the mystic Ocean tending . . . Song of the Universal . . . O public road . . . to know the universe itself as a road . . . along the grand roads of the universe . . . All, all, for immortality . . . it makes the whole coincide . . . I become part of that, whatever it is . . ."—such lines state the "omnific" principle behind the aggregates of the catalogues.

To such a cult of the "divine average," good will and good cheer sometimes come easy: "I love him, though I do not know him . . . I know not where they go; / But I know they go toward the best . . . surely the drift of them is something grand . . . illustrious every one . . . Great is Wealth—great is Poverty . . . Flaunt away, flags of all nations! . . . I believe materialism is true, and spiritualism is true—I reject no part . . . I do not see one imperfection in the universe . . . the venerealee is invited."* He thinks happily of "easily written, loose-fingered chords," and "the loose drift of character, the inkling through random types." He assures us, in hale and hearty camaraderie: "I turn the bridegroom out of bed, and stay with the bride myself"—nay more: "My voice is the wife's voice." His gusto suggests something like a cheerleader's at a chess tournament when he proclaims: "Hurrah for positive science! long live exact demonstration!" But the tactics are much subtler when, addressing a locomotive, he says: "Law of thyself complete, thine own track firmly holding."

In a poet capable of maintaining "this is Ocean's poem," a poet "aware of the mighty Niagara," the principle of joyously infused oneness can be centered in various terms of high generalization: "the greatness of Religion . . . the real and permanent grandeur of These States . . . efflux of the Soul . . . great City . . . transcendental Union . . . teeming Nation of nations . . . the immortal Idea . . . Sex" (which "contains all" . . . "every hour the semen of centuries")—all such subjects serve as variants on his theme of unified diversity. "Underneath all, Nativity" ("I swear I am charmed with nothing except nativity, / Men, women, cities, nations, are only beautiful from nativity"), by which he meant the individual being's uniqueness of identity ("singleness and normal simplicity and separation"). When he thinks of "Death, merged in the thought of materials," he swears "there is nothing but immortality!" When he "wander'd, searching among burial places," he "found that every place was a burial place." All "to the Ideal tendest"; "Only the good is universal"; "All swings around us. / I have the idea of all, and am all and believe in all"; "He resolves all tongues into his own."

In his prophetic role as "Chanter of Personality," he can use the Idea of Allness as justification for his claim to act as the spokesman for all: "I act as the tongue of you; / Tied in your mouth, in mine it begins to be loosened." Corresponding to "the great Idea, the idea of

---

* But not always. In *Song of the Open Road* we are told: "No diseas'd person, no rum-drinker or venereal taint is permitted here."

perfect and free individuals," an idea for which "the bard walks in advance," there are the many forms of idealized "appetite." These range from thoughts of a gallant and adventurous launching of "all men and women forward with me into the Unknown," to the notion of normal physical sensations programmatically made excessive, an abnormality of super-health: "Urge, and urge, and urge . . . complete abandonment . . . scattering it freely . . . athletic Democracy . . . ecstatic songs . . . the smoke of my own breath . . . the boundless impatience of restraint . . . unmitigated adoration . . . I inhale great draughts of space . . . tumbling on steadily, nothing dreading . . . give me the coarse and rank . . . fond of his sweetheart, relishing well his steak . . . aplomb in the midst of irrational things . . . turbulent, fleshy, sensual, eating, drinking, and breeding." In earlier versions of this last set honorifically describing himself, "turbulent" had been "disorderly." And we glimpse something of his rhetorical tactics when we recall that "I am he who goes through the streets" later became "I am he who walks the States." He gains concreteness in such inventions as "love-juice," "limitless limpid jets of love," and "life-lumps." Or analogies between the physical body and what J. C. Ransom has called the world's body are exploited in such statements as "Through you I drain the pent-up rivers of myself" (elsewhere he similarly speaks of "pent-up, aching rivers").

When we turn from the physical body and the world's body to the body politic, we note how such concretizing of the "democratic" code almost automatically vows the poet to imagery of a homosexual cast. For if Democracy is to be equated with "the manly love of comrades," and if such love is to be conceived *concretely*, in terms of bodily intimacy, such social "adhesiveness" ("the great rondure, the cohesion of all") that he advocates is almost necessarily matched by many expressions of "robust love" that would be alien to the typical heterosexual poet, as conditioned by our mores. And though the sex of his lover is not specified in the startling section 5 of *Song of Myself*, the many similarly motivated poems in *Calamus* give reason enough to assume that he is here writing of a male attachment, as with the "hugging and loving bed-fellow" of section 3 (though this passage may also be complicated by infantile memories of the mother). In any case, we should note, for what little it may be worth, that in *The Sleepers* Whitman associates the "onanist" with the color "gray," the same color with which he associates himself ("gray eyes" and "gray-necked"), while the "hermit thrush" singing in the "swamps" of the "Lilacs" poem is "gray-brown" (though "smoke" and "debris" here are also gray; and

there are other grays that are still further afield). The directest association of himself with an onanistic motive is in the last two lines of
"Spontaneous Me." Also, he uses a spiritual analogue (frequently encountered in devotional verse) when, concerning his literary motive,
he apostrophizes his tongue: "Still uttering—still ejaculating—canst
never cease this babble?"

As regards the poetic I, who would "promote brave soldiers," has
"voyagers' thoughts," would "strike up for a New World," is "he that
aches with amorous love," would "dilate you with tremendous breath,"
or "buoy you up": here his motives and motifs get their summarization
in his title of titles, *Leaves of Grass*. Accordingly, one direct way into
his verse is to ask what associations clearly cluster about these two
nouns, "leaves" and "grass" (which are related to each other as individuals are to the group, thus being in design like his term in the
Vistas, "ensemble-Individuality," though in that formula the order is
reversed). Here we are at the core of his personalizing tactics. And,
typically, it is in his *Song of Myself* that he specifically offers answers
to the question, "What is the grass?" (As indication that he would
here be the Answerer to a fundamental question, he tells us that it has
been asked by a child.) In section 6 of this poem, he offers several
definitions:

First, he says of grass: "I guess it must be the flag of my disposition, out of hopeful green stuff woven." Other references to "stuff"
in this poem are: "voices . . . of wombs and of the father-stuff";
"This day I am jetting the stuff of far more arrogant republics": "I am
. . . / Maternal as well as paternal, a child as well as a man, / Stuff'd
with the stuff that is coarse and stuff'd with the stuff that is fine." Elsewhere we have noted "I pour the stuff to start sons and daughters fit
for these States," and "these States with veins full of poetical stuff."
Interestingly enough, all other three references to "flag" in this poem
are in contrast with "hopeful green." There are "flag-tops . . . draped
with black muslin" to "guard some corpse"—and twice the word is used
as a verb, in the sense of "droop": "Did you fear some scrofula out
of the unflagging pregnancy?" and "The hounded slave that flags in
the race." (Note that "draped" is an ablaut form of "drooped" and
"dropt.")

Second: "Or I guess it is the handkerchief of the Lord, / A scented
gift and remembrancer designedly dropt, / Bearing the owner's name
. . ." We have noted no other references to handkerchiefs in Whitman, though there is always *Othello* in the offing! But the verb "dropt"

recalls the "drooped" and "dropt" of the "Lilacs" poem (which also refers to "inlooped flags with the cities draped in black") and since the matter of *scent* also links these two contexts, we shall wait for further leads here when we specifically deal with this theme. So far as the internal organization is concerned, by the way, we might note that the reference to the "owner's name" attains an enigmatic fulfillment near the end of the poem, when the poet decides that his motive is "without name . . . a word unsaid," though "To it the creation is the friend whose embracing awakes me."

Other meanings he offers are:

"I guess the grass is itself a child"; . . . "Or I guess it is a uni- form hieroglyphic, / . . . Growing among black folks as among white." Again, it seems like "the beautiful uncut hair of graves"—and as Whit- man frequently shuttles back and forth along the channel of affinity that links love and death or womb and tomb, his next stanza, beginning "Tenderly will I use you curling grass," contrives by quick transitions to go from "the breasts of young men" to "mothers' laps." In the fol- lowing stanza, grass is related to both "the white heads of old mothers" and "the colorless beards of old men," while a reference to "the faint red roofs of mouths" leads to the specifically poetic motive, in the men- tion of "uttering tongues."

Near the close of the poem (section 49) the theme of grass as the "hair of graves" is developed further ("O grass of graves"), while the connotations are generally of a maternal, or even obstetrical sort, in the references to the "bitter hug of mortality," the "elder-hand pressing," and the "accoucheur" who helps bring about "the relief and escape" through Death.

The scent theme figures here likewise, thanks to a bit of rhetorical alchemy. For after apostrophizing the "Corpse" as "good manure," the poet assures us: "but that does not offend me, / I smell the white roses sweet-scented and growing," whereat the associations, taking their lead from the vital connotations of the participle "growing," shift into quite a different order: "I reach to the leafy lips, I reach to the polish'd breasts of melons." And do we not find tonal vestiges of "leafy" in the two similar-sounding words of the next line: "And as to you Life I reckon you are the leavings of many deaths"?

To trail down the various uses of the verb "leave," in the light of the possibility that it may secondarily involve motives intrinsic to the noun "leaves," would take us on a longer journey than we could man- age now. But let us look at a few. Consider, for instance, in *Song of Myself*, section 3: "As the hugging and loving bed-fellow sleeps at my side through the night . . . / Leaving me baskets cover'd with white towels swelling the house with their plenty." In this context for "leaving," the hug is not overtly maternal, though the food connotations suggest that it may be secondarily so, quite as the "baskets" in this passage might correspond food-wise to the "polish'd breasts of melons" in the other. And similarly, in *Song of Myself*, section 6, an implicit food motive seems to guide the steps from "curling grass" to "the breasts of young men," and thence finally via "mothers" to "mouths," with a final turn from the nutriently oral to the poetically eloquent, in "uttering tongues." Yet, as regards "swelling the house with their plenty": we might recall that in "I Sing the Body Electric" we find the step from "love-flesh swelling and deliciously aching" to "jets of love hot and enormous," and two pages later: "There swells and jets a heart" (after talk of "blood" that might well bear study in connection with the talk of blood in the poem beginning "Trickle drops! my blue veins leaving! / O drops of me! trickle, slow drops, / Candid from me falling, drip, bleeding drops"). So the "hug" of Death or bed-fellows seems sometimes maternal, sometimes "democratic," or indeterminately something of both.

But our main intention at this point was to consider some more obvious cases where we might seem justified in adding the verb forms to our inquiry into the various major meanings of "leaves." Perhaps the perfect *pontificating* case is in *Starting from Paumanok*, where the line, "Take my leaves America" suggests something midway between "receive my offerings" and "put up with my constant departures." Or in so far as Whitman sometimes uses "blade" as a synonym for "leaf," there is another kind of bridge between noun and verb when, in "Scented Herbage of My Breast," in connection with male love, he says: "Emblematic and capricious blades I leave you." And before moving on, we'd like to consider one more context where the verb form seems quite relevant to our concerns. We have in mind the passage on Death, the "hug of mortality," the "sweet-scented," and Life as "the leavings of many deaths," a development that is immediately preceded by the lines (except for fifteen words):

> I find letters from God dropt in the street, and every one is sign'd by God's name,
> And I leave them where they are . . .

This is in section 48 of *Song of Myself*. Though this longest poem is sometimes entitled "Walt Whitman," we have said that there is in it a *problem of name* (that is, a problem of *essence*, of *fundamental motivation*; and we would base our position, naturally, upon the fact that, as the poet nears his windup, he centers upon the problem of locating a substance "without name"). But, relevantly reverting to the context where the word "name" first appears, we find it precisely in that passage (of section 6) where he speaks of the Lord's "scented" handkerchief, "bearing the owner's name," and "designedly dropt."

There are the many obvious places where the leaves are the leaves of books (a usage that fits well with a pun on utterance, in the notion of a tree's "uttering" leaves). A three-line poem in *Calamus* embodies this usage incidentally, in the course of a somewhat secretive confession :

> Here the frailest leaves of me and yet my strongest lasting,
> Here I shade and hide my thoughts, I myself do not expose them,
> And yet they expose me more than all my other poems.

The word "calamus" itself is apparently within the same orbit, and even allows us to watch "flag" for signs of similar meaning, since calamus is "sweet flag," of which our dictionary says: "The root has a pungent, aromatic taste, and is used in medicine as a stomachic ; the leaves have an aromatic odor, and were formerly used instead of rushes to strew on floors." Thus, we might assume that "calamus" is one of his "scent" words, though our incomplete reading has not as yet given us a clear title to this assumption. However, we can cite a one-page poem ("These I Singing in Spring") in which the mention of "calamus-root" accompanies such clearly scent-conscious references as "smelling the earthy smell," "lilac, with a branch of pine," and "aromatic cedar" (calamus-root here being specified as "the token of comrades"). Since "calamus" is the Latin word for "reed," we also dare note inklings of grassiness in the "reedy voice" of the hermit thrush that warbles through the "Lilacs" poem.

"Herbage" clearly belongs here—as in "Scented Herbage of My Breast" (though the subsequent references to "tomb-leaves," "body-leaves," "tall leaves," and "slender leaves . . . blossoms of my blood," while they are clear as radiations from the leaf motif, are somewhat vague in themselves). Herbage for grass is matched by feuillage for leaves ; and as judged by the assemblage of details in *Our Old Feuillage*, leaves can be any item that he includes in his surveys and poetic catalogues, here called "bouquets" ("Always . . . All sights . . . All characters . . ."; "Always the free range and diversity—always the continent of Democracy"; and "Encircling all, vast-darting up and wide, the American Soul, with equal hemispheres, one Love, one Dilation or Pride").

Leaves are sometimes called "blades"; and the blade of the broad-axe is called a "gray-blue leaf" (thereby adding the *gray* strand—and since the axe was "to be leaned and to lean on," we recall: "I lean and loafe at my ease observing a spear of summer grass"). Besides adding "spear" to our radiations, we note that "lean and loafe" are here attitudinally identical. But further, lo! not only is "loafe" tonally an ablaut form of "leaf"—change the unvoiced "f" to its voiced cognate, "v," and you have the close tonal proximity between "loafe" and "love."

"Leaves" and "grass" cross over into the scent category, in the reference to roots and leaves as "perfume," or in lines such as "The prairie-grass dividing, its special odor breathing," and "The sniff of green leaves and dry leaves . . . and of hay in the barn"—or the reference to "words simple as grass" that are "wafted with the odor of his body or breath."

Nowhere do we recall encountering such connotations as in the 129th Psalm, "Let them be as the grass upon the housetops, which withereth afore it groweth up"; or in Isaiah 40: "The grass withereth, the flower fadeth: because the spirit of the Lord bloweth upon it: surely the people is grass."

We should note two other major principles of unity:

First, there are the references to the "first," a common poetic and narrative device for the *defining of essence*. Perhaps the central example is his line: "I speak the password primeval, I give the sign of democracy." The more familiar we become with Whitman's vocabulary, the more condensed this line is felt to be. Identity is proclaimed quasi-temporally, in the word "primeval." Such firstness is further established in terms of the poetic I as spokesman for a public cause. But the more closely one examines the word "sign" in Whitman, the more one comes to realize that it has a special significance for him ranging from signs of God ("and every one is sign'd by God's name, / And I leave them where they are") to such signs as figure in a flirtation. (In "Among the Multitude," for instance: "I perceive one picking me out by secret and divine signs / . . . that one knows me. / Ah lover and perfect equal," as per the ambiguously "democratic" kind of equality especially celebrated in the *Calamus* poems.), "Password" is notable for merging one of his major verbs with the term that sums up his own specialty (elsewhere he has "passkey").

When proclaiming "a world primal again," he characteristically identifies it with the "new," the "expanding and swift," and the "turbulent." Another variant of such quasi-temporal firstness is in his term "nativity," as with "Underneath all, Nativity." And often references to the "child" serve the same reductive function (as with "Years looking backward resuming in answer to children").

Lines such as "Unfolded out of the folds of the woman, man comes unfolded," and "Out of the cradle endlessly rocking" reveal how readily such essentializing in terms of the "primal" can lead into the realm of the maternal (which may range from the sheer abstract principle of Union to the personally "electric," "magnetic," or "athletic"). And we might discern a "democratic" variant of the attitude implicit in the German epithet *wohlgeboren*, when he temporally defines his personal essence thus: "Starting from fish-shape Paumanok where I was born, / Well-begotten, and rais'd by a perfect mother."

There is a notable variant of the temporal idiom in "Crossing Brooklyn Ferry." For as the literal crossing of the river becomes symbolically a vision of crossing into the future, so the poet becomes a kind of essentializing past, defining the nature of his future readers. In "With Antecedents," we see how this temporal or narrative mode of defining essence can fit into the dialectics of *logical* priority (priority in the sense that the first premise of a syllogism can be considered prior to the second premise). For while, as his very title indicates, he is concerned with the temporally prior, he reduces his temporal sequence in turn to terms of "all" when he says: "We stand amid time beginningless and endless, we stand amid evil and good, / All swings around us."

In his *Song of the Open Road*, which calls upon us continually to "reach" and "pass," and "to merge all in the travel they tend to," he uses a reverse kind of temporal priority; namely: seniority. "Old age, calm, expanded, broad with the haughty breadth of the universe, / Old age, flowing free with the delicious near-by freedom of death." (The broad-breadth pair here could lead us into his notable breast-breath set.) But with the subject of Death, we come upon another kind of summing up, since it names the direction in which the "ever-tending" is headed. ("Tend" is as typical a Whitman word as "pass," though it occurs much less frequently.) So, let us consider Whitman's poetizing of Death. But since Death is the Great Positive-Seeming Negative, perhaps we might best consider it with relation to the poet's use of the negative in general.

The incidence of negatives is probably highest in the poems of the *Calamus* period; at least, in many places here they come thick and fast. There is almost an orgy of not's and nor's in "Not Heaving from My Ribb'd Breast Only," as sixteen of the poem's seventeen lines so begin, while one line contains a second. Since the poem is composed of a single periodic sentence about "adhesiveness" (the "pulse of my life"), we should certainly be justified in asking whether there may be a substantive relation in these poems between the negative and the resolve to celebrate democracy with songs of "manly attachment." (See also particularly in this same series: "Not Heat Flames Up and Consumes"; "City of Orgies"; "No Labor-Saving Machine"; or the way in which a flat "no" serves as fulcrum in "What Think You I Take My Pen in Hand?")

It might also be worth noting that the *Calamus* theme of the "subtle electric fire that for your sake is playing within me" produces two significant and quite appealing instances of anacoluthon: "City whom that I have lived and sung in your midst will one day make you illustrious," and "O you whom I often and silently come where you are that I may be with you." (We mention anacoluthon here because, tentatively, though not for certain, we incline to believe that the figure indicates a certain deviousness in thinking, hence may remotely indicate a "problematical" motive.)

A more orthodox strategy of deflection (almost a *diplomacy*) is to be seen in another poem of the *Calamus* series, "Earth, My Likeness." Beginning on the theme of the analogy between the poet's body and the earth as a body, the poet then avows a questionable motive in himself, after figuratively attributing a like motive to the earth:

> I now suspect there is something fierce in you eligible to burst forth,
>
> For an athlete is enamour'd of me, and I of him,
>
> But toward him there is something fierce and terrible in me eligible to burst forth,
>
> I dare not tell it in words, not even in these songs.*

---

* The lines contain many notable terms. First, since they twice say "eligible," we might remember the connotations here when we come upon the word elsewhere. Thus, when winding up *Our Old Feuillage*, Whitman writes: "Whoever you are! how can I but offer you divine leaves, that you also be eligible as I am?" Or in *By Blue Ontario's Shore*, see "All is eligible to all." And recalling the "lessons" on which *Democratic Vistas* began, note in *Starting from Paumanok*: "I sat studying at the feet of the great masters, / Now if eligible O that the great masters might return and study me." The repetition of "fierce" might recall the "fierce old mother" and "savage old mother" of "Out of the Cradle Endlessly Rocking." Also "liberty songs" were fierce. The poem gives us some specific meanings for "athlete," to be remembered even though the word can be extended to an "athletic matron." And the movement ends in the negative, with relation to his own verse.

In *Song of Myself* (section 44) there is an absolute negative, identified with a "first":

> Afar down I see the huge first Nothing, I know I was even there,
> I waited unseen and always, and slept through the lethargic mist,
> And took my time, and took no hurt from the fetid carbon.
>
> Long I was hugg'd close—long and long.

Immediately after, the thought is developed in terms of the maternal. For instance: "Cycles ferried my cradle," and "Before I was born out of my mother generations guided me," lines that overlap upon even the sheer titles of *Crossing Brooklyn Ferry* and "Out of the Cradle Endlessly Rocking." The word "hugg'd" might remind us of the previously quoted reference to "the hugging and loving bed-fellow . . . / Leaving me baskets," etc. (section 3). Or there was the "hug of mortality" in section 49, and the death-smell that "does not offend me" and was quickly replaced by talk of the "sweet-scented."

Section 12 in *Starting from Paumanok* has some interesting involvements with the negative. First the poet addresses his femme, Democracy. In her name he will make both the "songs of passion" and the "true poem of riches." He will "effuse egotism," and will show that male and female are equal.

We might note that such equality of sex could mean one thing as applied to the body politic, but something quite different if applied to the individual personality. For within the individual personality, an "equality" of "male" and "female" motives could add up to an ambivalence of the *androgynous* sort, as it would not, strictly in the realm of politics. Yet we must also bear in mind the fact that, however close language may be to the persuasions and poetics of sexual courtship, language as such is nonsexual; and in so far as motivational perturbations arising from purely *linguistic* sources become personalized in terms of any real or imagined distinctions between "male" and "female," such sexual-seeming differentiations should be inadequate to the case; hence, any purely linguistic situations that happened to be stated in sexual terms (involving either sexual differentiations or sexual mergers) should have elements that could be but *prophetically glimpsed* beyond a terminology formed by sexual analogies.

For instance, though language necessarily has a realm of dialectical resources wholly extrinsic to sexuality, there is the ironic linguistic fact that concrete bisexual imagery may be inevitable, if a poet, let us say, would give us not at one time the image of *mother* and at another the image of *father*, but would rather seek to localize in concrete imagery the idea of *parent*. At the very least, thinking of such a linguistic embarrassment along psychoanalytic lines, we might expect some kind of merger or amalgam like that in Whitman's exclamation: "Mother! with subtle sense severe, with the naked sword in your hand." (And after the analogy of "spears" of grass, we might well have swords of grass, too, not forgetting the naked broad-axe. Further, a poet given to homosexual imagery might well, when writing of his verbal art, glimpse the wholly nonsexual quandaries that lie in the bed of language, far beyond any and all sociopolitical relations.)*

But we were on the subject of the negatives in section 12 of *Starting from Paumanok*. Immediately after the poet has proclaimed the equality of male and female, and has vowed that he will prove "sexual organs and acts" to be "illustrious," the negatives come piling in. He will show that "there is no imperfection in the present, and can be none in the future," and that "nothing can happen more beautiful than death." The next stanza has a negative in four of its five verses, and the positive line is introduced by a disjunctive conjunction:

> I will not make poems with reference to parts,
> But I will make poems, songs, thoughts, with reference to ensemble,
> And I will not sing with reference to a day, but with reference to all days,
> And I will not make a poem nor the least part of a poem but has reference to the soul,
> Because having look'd at the objects of the universe, I find there is no one nor any particle of one but has reference to the soul.

Whereas the Whitman negative, at one extreme, seems to involve the notions of No-No that trouble the scruples of "manly love" (scru-

---

* See *Der Monat*, Juni 1954, Heft 69: *Die Alten Ägypter*, by J. A. Wilson, page 277: *Ein anderer, irdischerer Text macht aus der Erschaffung von Schu und Tefnut einen Akt der Selbstbefleckung Atums—ein deutlicher Versuch, mit dem Problem fertig zu werden, wie ein Gott allein, ohne dazugehörige Göttin, etwas zeugen soll.* And on page 280, returning to the theme of a creation *aus einer Selbstbefleckung des Schöpfergottes,* a creation made *"aus seinem Samen und seinen Fingern,"* the author next says (and we consider this a thoroughly substantial association): *Wir sahen ja schon, wie das Aussprechen eines Namens an sich ein Schöpfungsakt ist.* We have many times been struck by the fact that the creative word could be called parthenogenesis or *Selbstbefleckung,* depending on whichever sexual analogies the analogizer preferred; but this is the first time we ever encountered so heroic a version of such thinking. And we are particularly struck by the writer's turn from the subject of this self-involved physical act on the part of a wholly independent god to the subject of creation by verbal fiat.

ples that somehow connect with thoughts of the maternal and, of course, with the problem of his identity, or "nativity," as a poet), in the above quotation we see how such matters fade into purely technical considerations. For if the *particulars* of life are positive, then the "ensemble" or "soul" would be correspondingly negative; or if you considered the "ensemble" positive, then the "parts" would be negative (as with Spinoza's principle: *omnis determinatio est negatio*). Or in a fluctuant medium such as Whitman's, where the issues need not be strictly drawn, the talk of parts and wholes may merely call forth a general aura of negativity. However, once we consider this problem from the standpoint of the distinction between positive and negative, we should note the dialectical resources whereby, above the catalogues of positive details that characteristically make up so many of his poems, there should hover some summarizing principle—and this principle would be "negative," at least in the sense that no single detail could be it, though each such positive detail might partitively stand for it, or be infused with its spirit. (The problem is analogous to that of negative theology.)

When the technical principles of positive and negative are projected into their moralistic counterparts (as good and evil), the poet can assert by the doubling of negatives, as in "I will show that there is no imperfection." And if you will agree that death is negative (in so far as it is the privation of life), then you will note double negativity lurking in the statements that "nothing can happen more beautiful than death," or "Copulation is no more rank to me than death is."

Sometimes the *principle* of negativity is present, but in a positive-seeming statement that is really a denial of a social negative, as with "the bowels sweet and clean," or "perfect and clean the genitals previously jetting." Or here is a line that runs heretically counter to vast sums expended in the advertising of deodorants for people who think that their vague sense of personal guilt is to be eliminated by purely material means: "the scent of these armpits aroma finer than prayer." In keeping with this pattern, he can also celebrate the "joy of death," likening it to the discharging of excrement ("My voided body nothing more to me, returning to the purifications"). Similarly, farther afield, as though boasting of virtues, he can tell of the vices that were "not wanting" in him ("the wolf, the snake, the hog," among others). For he "will make the poem of evil also," for "I am myself just as much evil as good, and my nation is"—whereat, expanding further, "and I say there is in fact no evil." Accordingly, "none can be interdicted, / None but are accepted."

At one point in *Song of the Open Road* he formulates the principle in general terms, in ways suggesting Hegel: "It is provided in the essence of things that from any fruition of success, no matter what, shall come forth something to make a greater struggle necessary," a principle that could provide good grounds for feeling downcast, if one were so inclined. Elsewhere, "after reading Hegel," he avows: "the vast all that is called Evil I saw hastening to merge itself and become lost and dead." And in keeping with the same design, he could praise the earth because "It grows such sweet things out of such corruptions."

In sum, Whitman would programmatically make all days into a kind of permanent Saturnalian revel, though celebrating not a golden age of the past, but rather the present in terms of an ideal future. And, in poetically personalizing his program, he "promulges" democracy in terms of a maternal allness or firstness and fraternal universality ambiguously intermingling in a death hug that presents many central problems for the patient pedestrian analyzer of The Good Gray Poet's terminology.

But when we remind ourselves that the Roman Saturnalia traditionally involved a ritualistic reversal of roles, with the slaves and servants playing as masters for a day while the masters playfully took orders, we wonder whether the ironic bitterness of Whitman's poem, "Respondez! Respondez!" (first published in 1856 as "Poem of the Proposition of Nakedness") might be studied as a kind of Saturnalia-in-reverse.

"Let the slaves be masters! let the masters become slaves!" he exhorts—but this call to the answerer is phrased rather in the accents of outrage. "Let the cow, the horse, the camel, the garden-bee—let the mudfish, the lobster, the mussel, eel, the sting-ray, and the grunting pig-fish—let these, and the like of these, be put on a perfect equality with man and woman!"

In this almost splutteringly ferocious poem, the nation is surveyed wholly without benefit of his normal "spiritualization":

> Stifled, O days, O lands! in every public and private corruption!
> Smothered in thievery, impotence, shamelessness, mountain-high;
> Brazen effrontery, scheming, rolling like ocean's waves around and upon you, O my days! my lands! . . .
> —Let the theory of America still be management, caste, comparison! (Say! what other theory would you?)

And so on, and so on. "Let there be money, business, imports, exports, custom, authority, precedents, pallor, dyspepsia, smut, ignorance, unbelief!"

As for this sullen poem in which he stylistically turns his usual promulgations upside down, we perhaps have here the equivalent of such reversal as marks the mystic state of "accidie." In any case, of all his negatives, this poem would seem to have been one that carried him quite outside his characteristic literary role. It shows how very harsh things could seem to him, in those days, when for a moment he let himself look upon the conditions of his day without the good aid of his futuristic IDEA.

III. LILACS

Having considered Whitman's political philosophy in general, and the general way in which he personalized his outlook by translation into the rapt editorializing of his verse, we would here narrow our concerns to a close look at one poem, his very moving dirge, "When Lilacs Last in the Dooryard Bloom'd," perhaps the poem of his in which policies and personalizations came most nearly perfectly together.

The programmatic zestfulness that marks Whitman's verse as strongly as Emerson's essays encountered two challenges for which it had not been originally "promulged": the Civil War, and the valetudinarianism forced upon him by his partial paralytic stroke in 1873.

Before these developments, his stylistics of "spiritualization" had provided him with a categorical solution for the problem of evil as he saw it. Except for the outlaw moment of "Respondez! Respondez!" (or its much briefer form, "Reversals") his futuristic idealizing could readily transform all apprehensions into promises, and could discern a unitary democratic spirit behind any aggregate of natural or manmade places or things that added up to national power and prowess. This same principle was embodied in the random samplings that made up his poetic surveys and catalogues (which do impart a note of exhilaration to his text, even though one inclines to skim through them somewhat as when running the eye down the column of a telephone directory). And whatever guilt was left unresolved by his code could be canceled by the accents of perfervid evangelism (notably in his celebrating of "adhesiveness").

But since the entire scheme was based upon an ideal of all-pervasive and almost promiscuous Union, the motives of secession that culminated in the Civil War necessarily filled him with anguish. And even many of the inferior poems in *Drum-Taps* become urgent and poignant, if read as the diary of a man whose views necessarily made him most sensitive to the dread of national dismemberment. Here, above all, was the development in history itself which ran harshly counter to the basic promises in which his poetry had invested. He reproaches not himself but "America": "Long, too long . . . / you learned from joys and prosperity only." And, in slightly wavering syntax, he says the need is henceforth "to learn from crises of anguish."

Yet in one notable respect, his doctrines had prepared him for this trial. In contrast with the crudity of mutual revilement and incrimination that marks so many contemporary battles between the advocates of Rightist and Leftist politics, Whitman retained some of the spontaneous gallantry toward the enemy that sometimes (as in *Chevy-Chase*) gives the old English-Scottish border ballads their enlightening moral nobility. And whatever problematical ingredients there may have been in his code of love as celebrated in the *Calamus* poems, these motives were sacrificially transformed in his work and thoughts as wound-dresser ("I have nourished the wounded and soothed many a dying soldier" . . . "Upon this breast has many a dying soldier leaned to breathe his last" . . . "Many a soldier's loving arms about this neck have cross'd and rested, / Many a soldier's kiss dwells on these bearded lips").

Similarly, when ill health beset him, though it went badly with one who had made a particular point of celebrating the body at the height of its physical powers, here too he had a reserve to draw upon. For his cult of death as a kind of all-mother (like the sea) did allow him a place in his system for infirmities. Further, since death was that condition toward which all life *tends*, he could write of old age, "I see in you the estuary that enlarges and spreads itself grandly as it pours in the great sea"—and though this is nearly his briefest poem, it is surely as *expansionist* a view as he ever proclaimed in his times of broad-axe vigor. We have already mentioned his new-found sympathy with the fallen redwood tree. Other identifications of this sort are imagined in his lines about an ox tamer, and about a locomotive in winter (he now wrote "recitatives").

As for the lament on the death of Lincoln: here surely was a kind of Grand Resolution, done at the height of his powers. Embodied in it, there is a notable trinity of sensory images, since the three major interwoven symbolic elements—evening star, singing bird, and lilac— compose a threeness of sight, sound, and scent respectively. Also, perhaps they make a threeness of paternal, filial, and maternal respectively. Clearly, the star stands for the dead hero; and the "hermit" bird, "warbling a song," just as clearly stands for the author's poetizing self.

But whereas vicarious aspects of star and bird are thus defined within the poem itself, we believe that the role of the lilac is better understood if approached through an inquiry into the subject of scent in general, as it figures in Whitman's idiom.

In the section on *Vistas*, we put much store by the passage where, after referring to "that indescribable perfume of genuine womanhood," Whitman next speaks of his mother, then proceeds to describe an elderly lady, a "resplendent person, down on Long Island." We consider this set of steps strongly indicative, particularly in so far as many other passages can be assembled which point in the same direction. And though Whitman's associations with scent radiate beyond the orbit of the feminine, maternal, and grandmotherly, we believe that his terms for scent have their strongest motivational jurisdiction in this area, with the *Calamus* motive next.

In this Lincoln poem, the lilac is explicitly called "the perfume strong I love." The sprigs from the lilac bushes ("to perfume the grave of him I love") are not just for this one coffin, but for "coffins all." And the Death figured in such lilac-covered coffins is called a "Dark Mother." In "Out of the Cradle Endlessly Rocking," where there is the same identification of the maternal and the deathy, the development is built about the account of a solitary "he-bird . . . warbling" for his lost mate, quite as with the mournful warbling of the hermit thrush—and the incident is said to have taken place "When the lilac-scent was in the air and Fifth-month grass was growing."

The cedars and pines in the "recesses" of the swamp where the hermit thrush is singing are also explicitly included in the realm of scent, as evidenced by the lines: "From the fragrant cedars and the ghostly pines"; "Clear in the freshness moist and the swamp-perfume"; "There in the fragrant pines and the cedars dusk and dim." See also, in *Starting from Paumanok*, that poem of his origins and of his femme Democracy: having heard "the hermit thrush from the swamp-cedars, / Solitary, singing in the West, I strike up for a New World." But it is the lilac that holds the poet "with mastering odor," as he says in the Lincoln poem.

In another poem, *A Broadway Pageant* (and one should think also of broad-axe and broad breast), there is a passage that clearly brings out the identification between scent and the maternal, though in this case the usage is somewhat ambiguous in attitude, whereas by far the great majority of references to scent in Whitman are decidedly on the favorable side: "The Originatress comes, / The nest of languages, the bequeather of poems, the race of eld, / Florid with blood, pensive, rapt with musings, hot with passion, / Sultry with perfume." (His word "florid" here could be correlated with a reference to "Florida per-fumes," in a poem on Columbia, "the Mother of All.") In this same poem, near the end, there is a passage about "the all-mother" and "the long-off mother" which develops from the line: "The box-lid is but perceptibly open'd, nevertheless the perfume pours copiously out of the whole box." Psychoanalytically, the point about identification here could be buttressed by the standard psychoanalytic interpretation of "box," and thus perhaps by extending the same idea to the coffin—but we would prefer to stress merely the sequence of steps in this passage itself, while noting that the terms for derivation ("out of") take us once again back to the "Cradle" poem.

Consider also this passage, near the windup of *Song of Myself*:

> The past and present wilt—I have fill'd them, emptied them,
> And proceed to fill my next fold of the future.
>
> Listen up there! what have you to confide to me?
> Look in my face while I snuff the sidle of evening . . .

Does not "snuff the sidle" here suggest the picture of a youngster nosing against the side of the evening, as were the evening an adult, with a child pressing his face against its breast? In any case, "fold" is a notable word in Whitman, with its maternal connotations obvious in the line where the syllable is repeated almost like an *idée fixe*: "Unfolded out of the folds of the woman, man comes unfolded," an expression that also has the "out of" construction. Another refer-ence, "Endless unfolding of words of ages," leads into talk of accept-ance ("I accept Reality and dare not question it, / Materialism first and last imbuing")—and two lines later he speaks of "cedar and branches of lilac." Recall also the traditional association of the feminine with matter (as in Aristotle). In the "Lilacs" poem, immediately before the words "dark mother," death is called "cool-enfolding."

In one of the *Calamus* poems, a reference to "perfume" follows immediately after the line, "Buds to be unfolded on the old terms," and there are other lines that extend the area of the perfume beyond the feminine and maternal to the realm of manly adhesiveness, and to his poetic development in general, as in "In Cabin'd Ships at Sea": "Bear forth to them folded my love, (dear mariners, for you I fold it here in every leaf)."

There are many other references, direct and indirect, which we could offer to establish the maternal as a major element in the lilac theme. But we believe that these should be enough to prove the point.

Imagine, then, a situation of this sort:

A poet has worked out a scheme for identifying his art with the ideal of a democratic "empire" that he thinks of as a matrix, an All-Mother, a principle of unity bestowing its sanctions upon a strong love of man for man, an "adhesiveness" generally "spiritual," but also made concrete in imagery of "athletic" physical attachment. Quite as God is conceived as both efficient cause and final cause, so this poet's unitary principle is identified with both a source from which he was "unfolded" (the maternal origins "out of" which his art derived) and an end toward which he "ever-tended" (death, that will receive him by "enfolding" him, thus completing the state of "manifold ensemble" through which he had continually "passed," by repeatedly "coming" and "departing"). A beloved democratic hero has died—and the lyric commemoration of this tragic death will be the occasion of the poem.

How then would he proceed, within the regular bounds of his methods and terminology, to endow this occasion with the personal and impersonal *dimensions* that give it scope and resonance? (For a good poem will be not just one strand, but the interweaving of strands.)

Note, first, that the poem involves several situations. There is the commemorated situation, the death of the hero, as made specific in the journey of the coffin on its last journey. There is the immediate situation of the commemorating poet, among a set of sensory perceptions that he associates, for us, with the hero's death. There is the national scene that he can review, after the fashion of his catalogues, when charting the journey of the coffin (and when radiating into other details loosely connected with this). Near the end, a national scene that had *preceded* the hero's death will be recalled (the time of civil war, or intestine strife, that had accounted historically for the tragic sacrifice). And in the offing, "over-arching" all, there is the notion of an ultimate scene (life, death, eternity, and a possibility of interrelationships in terms of which immediate sensory images can seem to take on an element of the marvelous, or transcendent, through standing for correspondences beyond their nature as sheerly physical objects). The reader shifts back and forth spontaneously, almost unawares, among these different scenes, with their different orders of motivation, the interpenetration of which adds subtlety and variety to the poem's easy simplicity.

The three major *sensory* images are star, bird, and bush (each with its own special surroundings: the darkening Western sky for the "drooping" star, the "recesses" of the swamp for the "hermit" bird, the dooryard for the lilac, with its loved strong perfume—and for all three, the evening in "ever-returning spring"). As regards their correspondences with things beyond their nature as sheerly sensory images: the star stands for the dead loved hero (in a scheme that, as with so much of the Wagnerian nineteenth century, readily equates love and death). The bird crosses over, to a realm beyond its sheerly sensuous self, by standing for the poet who mourns, or celebrates, the dead hero (while also ambiguously mourning or celebrating himself).

And what of the third image, the scent of lilac? It fits the occasion in the obvious sense that it blooms in the springtime and is a proper offering for coffins. And though it is from a realm more material, more earthy, than sight or sound, it has a strong claim to "spirit" as well, since scent is *breathed*. (Passages elsewhere in Whitman, such as "sweet-breathed," "inhaling the ripe breath of autumn," and "the shelves are crowded with perfumes, / I breathe the fragrance," remind us that references to breathing can be secondarily in the scent orbit, and often are in Whitman's idiom.)

Though, in the lore of the Trinity, the Father is equated with power, the Son with wisdom, and the Holy Spirit with love, it is also said that these marks of the three persons overlap. And similarly, in this trinity (of star, bird, and bush) there are confusions atop the distinctions. In so far as the bird stands for the poet whose art (according to the *Vistas*) was to teach us lessons, the bird would correspond to the son, and wisdom. The star, in standing for the dead Lincoln, would surely be an equivalent of the father, implying power in so far as Lincoln had been a national democratic leader. Yet the nearest explicit attribution of power, the adjective "strong," is applied only in connection with the *lilac*, which would be analogous to the third person of the trinity, the holy spirit (with the notable exception that we would treat it as *maternal*, whereas the Sanctus Spiritus is, *grammatically* at least, imagined after the analogy of the masculine, though often surrounded by imagery that suggests maternal, quasi-Mariolatrous connotations).

The relation of lilac to love is in the reference to "heart-shaped leaves." Since the evening star is unquestionably Venus, the love theme is implicitly figured, though ambiguously, in so far as Venus is feminine, but is here the sign of a dead *man*. As for the "solitary" thrush, who sings "death's outlet song of life," his "carol of death" is a love song at least secondarily, in so far as love and death are convertible terms.

Also, in so far as the bird song is explicitly said to be a "tallying chant" that matches the poet's own "thought of him I love," the love motif is connected with it by this route.

But the words, "song of the bleeding throat," remind us of another motive here, more *autistic*, intrinsic to the self, as might be expected of a "hermit" singer. Implicit in the singing of the thrush, there is the theme most clearly expressed perhaps in these earlier lines, from *Calamus*:

> Trickle drops! my blue veins leaving!
> O drops of me! trickle, slow drops,
> Candid from me falling, drip, bleeding drops,
> From wounds made to free you whence you were prison'd,
> From my face, from my forehead and lips,
> From my breast, from within where I was conceal'd, press forth
>   red drops, confession drops,
> Stain every page, stain every song I sing, every word I say,
>   bloody drops,
> Let them know your scarlet heat, let them glisten,
> Saturate them with yourself all ashamed and wet,
> Glow upon all I have written or shall write, bleeding drops,
> Let it all be seen in your light, blushing drops.

Do we not here find the theme of utterance proclaimed in and for itself, yet after the analogy of violence done upon the self?

Regrettably, we cannot pause to appreciate the "Lilacs" poem in detail. But a few terministic considerations might be mentioned. There is the interesting set of modulations, for instance, in the series: night, black murk, gray debris, dark-brown fields, great cloud darkening the land, draped in black, crepe-veiled, dim-lit, netherward black of the night, gray smoke, gray-brown bird out of the dusk, long black trail, swamp in the dimness, shadowy cedars, dark mother, dusk and dim— all in contrast with the "lustrous" star. (If you will turn to *Song of Myself*, section 6, you will find the "dark mother" theme interestingly foreshadowed in the "dark . . . darker . . . dark" stanza that serves as a transition from "mothers' laps" to "uttering tongues.") And noting the absence of Whitman's distance-blue, we find that he has moved into the more solemn area of lilac, purple, and violet. Note also the spring-sprig modulation.

There are many devices for merging the components. At times, for instance, the swampy "recesses" where the bird is singing are described in terms of scent. Or sight and scent are intermingled when "fragrant cedars" are matched with "ghostly pines" at one point, and "fragrant pines" are matched with "cedars dusk and dim" at another. And of course, there is the notable closing merger, "Lilac and star and bird twined with the chant of my soul," a revision of his "trinity" in the opening stanzas, where the bird does not figure at all, the third of the three being the poet's "thought of him I love."

Prophesying after the event, of course, we could say that the bird had figured *implicitly* from the very first, since the bird duplicates the poet, though this duplex element will not begin to emerge until section 4, where the bird is first mentioned. But once the bird has been introduced, much effectiveness derives from the poem's return, at intervals, to this theme, which is thus astutely released and developed. One gets the feel of an almost frenzied or orgiastic outpouring, that has never stopped for one moment, and somehow even now goes unendingly on.

One gets no such clear sense of progression in the poem as when, say, reading *Lycidas*. But if pressed, we could offer grounds for contending that section 13 (the mathematical center of the poem) is the point of maximum internality. For instance, whereas in sections 4 and 9, the thrush is "warbling" *in* the swamp, here the song is said to come *from* the swamps, *from* the bushes, *out of* the dusk, *out of* the cedars and pines (a prepositional form which we, of course, associate with the maternal connotations it has in the opening stanzas of "Out of the Cradle Endlessly Rocking"). Thus, one might argue that there is a crucial change of direction shaping up here. Also, whereas section 4 had featured the sound of the bird's song, and section 9 had added the star along with talk of the bird's song, in section 13 we have bird, star, and lilac, all three (plus a paradox which we may ascribe at least in part to the accidental limitations of English—for whereas we feel positive in associating lilac with the feminine or maternal, the poet writes of the "mastering" odor with which the lilac holds him).

We could say that the theme of the cradle song, or "Death Carol" (that follows, after a brief catalogue passage) had been implicitly introduced in the "from's" and "out of's" that characterize the first stanza of section 13. But in any case, a clear change of direction follows this movement, with its theme of death as "dark mother." And since we would make much of this point, let us pause to get the steps clear:

As regards the purely sensory imagination, the theme (of the "Death Carol" as cradle song) is developed in the spirit of such words as soothe, serenely, undulate, delicate, soft, floating, loved, laved. And whereas there is no sensory experience suggested in the words "praise! praise! praise!" surely they belong here wholly because of the poet's desire to use whatever associations suggest total relaxation, and because of the perfect freedom that goes with the act of genuine, unstinted praise, when given without ulterior purpose, from sheer spontaneous delight.

What next, then, after this moment of farthest yielding? Either the poem must end there (as it doesn't), or it must find some proper aftermath. The remaining stanzas, as we interpret them, have it in their favor that they offer a solution of this problem.

As we see it, a notable duality of adjustment takes place here (along lines somewhat analogous to the biologists' notion of the correspondence between ontogenetic and phylogenetic evolution, with regard to the stages that the individual foetus passes through, in the course of its development).

In brief, there are certain matters of recapitulation to be treated, purely within the conditions of the poem; but if these are to be wholly vital, there must be a kind of *new act* here, even thus late in the poem, so far as the momentum of the poet is concerned. And we believe that something of the following sort takes place:

In imagining death as maternal, the poet has imagined a state of ideal infantile or intra-uterine bliss. Hence, anything experienced *after* that stage will be like the emergence of the child from its state of Eden into the world of conflict. Accordingly, after the "Death Carol," the poet works up to a recital in terms of armies, battle flags, the "torn and bloody," "debris," etc. Strictly within the conditions of the poem, all these details figure as recollections of the Civil War, with its conditions of strife which accounted historically for the hero's death. But from the standpoint of this section's place *after* the imagining of infantile contentment, all such imagery of discord is, in effect, the recapitulation of a human being's emergence into the intestine turmoils of childhood and adolescence.

After this review of discord, there is a recapitulation designed to bring about the final mergings, fittingly introduced by the repetition of Whitman's password, "passing." There had been much merging already. Now, in the gathering of the clan, there is a final assertion of merger, made as strong and comprehensive as possible. The "hermit song" is explicitly related to the "tallying song" of the poet's "own soul." The "gray-brown bird" is subtly matched by the "silver face" of the star. Our previous notion about the possible pun in "leaves" (as noun and verb) comes as near to substantiation as could be, in the line: "Passing, I leave thee lilac with heart-shaped leaves." There is a comradely holding of hands.

So, with the thought of the hero's death, all is joined: "the holders holding my hand"; "lilac and star and bird twined with the chant of my soul"; "and this for his dear sake," a sacrifice that ends on the line, "The fragrant pines and cedars dusk and dim"—nor should we forget that the sounds issuing from there came from the "recesses" of the "swamp-perfume."*

The first line of a Whitman poem is usually quite different rhythmically from the lines that follow. The first line generally has the formal rhythm of strict verse, while even as early as the second line he usually turns to his typical free-verse style. (*Song of the Broad-Axe* is an exception to the rule, as it opens with no less than six lines that do not depart far from the pattern: long-short/ long-short/ long-short/ long, as set by the verse: "Weapon, shapely, naked, wan.") We copied out a batch of first lines, just to see how they would look if assembled all in one place, without reference to the kind of line that characterizes most notably the poet's catalogues. When reading them over, we noted that they are so much of a piece, and gravitate so constantly about a few themes, one might make up a kind of Whitman Medley, composed of nothing but first lines, without a single alteration in their wording. Here is one version of such an arrangement. It is offered as a kind of critical satyr-play, to lighten things after the tragic burden of our long analysis:

First O Songs for a Prelude

Lo, the unbounded sea!
Flood-tide below me! I see you face to face!
In cabined ships at sea,

* Five lines from the end, the expression "Comrades mine and I in the midst," restating in slight variation the words of section 14, "I in the middle with companions," might be used as an indication of the way in which the poet's terms radiate. In *Calamus* there is a poem that also has the expression, "I in the middle." One will also find there "lilac with a branch of pine," "aromatic cedar," the themes of singing and plucking (to match "A sprig with its flower I break"), and a reference to "the spirits of friends dead or alive." In *A Broadway Pageant*, there also appears the expression "in the middle." But just as the other usage had been a bridge into the theme of comradely attachment, here the context is definitely in the maternal orbit. This same stanza contains the reference to the perfume that "pours copiously out of the whole box," and "venerable Asia, the all-mother." In the "Lilacs" poem, the theme of copious pouring is distributed differently. In section 13, the bird is told to "pour" its song; in section 7, the idea is transferred to the breaking of the lilac: "Copious I break, I break the sprigs from the bushes, / With loaded arms I come pouring for you"—whereat again we would recall that the first reference to the "shy and hidden bird," with its "song of the bleeding throat," followed the line, "A sprig with its flower I break."

Out of the cradle endlessly rocking,
Over the Western sea hither from Niphon come
As I ebb'd with the ocean of life,
Facing west from California's shore,
Give me the splendid silent sun with all his beams full-dazzling.

O to make the most jubilant song!
A song for occupations!
A song of the rolling earth, and of words according,
I hear America singing, the varied carols I hear.
These I singing in spring collect for lovers,
Trickle drops! my blue veins leaving!
America always! Always our old feuillage!
Come, said the Muse,
Come my tan-faced children.

(Now list to my morning's romanza, I tell the signs of the
    Answerer.
An old man bending I come upon new faces,
Spirit whose work is done—spirit of dreadful hours!
Rise, O days, from your fathomless deeps, till you loftier, fiercer
    sweep.)

As I pondered in silence,
Starting from fish-shape Paumanok where I was born,
From pent-up aching rivers;
As I lay with my head in your lap camerado,
Thou who has slept all night upon the storm;
Vigil strange I kept on the field one night,
On the beach at night
By blue Ontario's shore.

I sing the body electric,
Weapon shapely, naked, wan,
Scented herbage of my breast,
Myself and mine gymnastic ever,
Full of life now, compact visible,
I celebrate myself and sing myself;
Me imperturbe, standing at ease in Nature.

On journeys through the States we start,
Among the men and women, the multitude,
In paths untrodden,
The prairie grass dividing, its special odor breathing—
Not heaving from my ribbed breast only,
Afoot and light-hearted I take to the open road.

You who celebrate bygones,
Are you the new person drawn toward me?
Whoever you are, I fear you are walking the walks of dreams.
Behold this swarthy face, these gray eyes;
Passing stranger! you do not know how longingly I look upon
    you.

Respondez! Respondez!
Here, take this gift—
Come, I will make the continent indissoluble.
O take my hand, Walt Whitman!
As Adam early in the morning
To the garden anew ascending.

Walt Whitman: Impressionist Prophet

OF THE various views of the nature and function of poetry which have been held over the ages, perhaps the two most diametrically opposed to each other are the prophetic and the confessional—the view that poetry should deal with some large moral theme which is, in Milton's phrase, "doctrinal to a nation," and the view that poetry represents the poet communing with himself, expressing his most secret and personal impressions and emotions. The epic urge, the desire to deal with grand, public themes, to focus the traditions of a civilization through a broad pattern of heroic action, is bound up with the first view, and the lyrical urge, to express oneself and exploit one's emotional autobiography, with the second. There is, of course, a rich middle ground between these two extremes, and most poets of any stature have moved freely between them. Yet on the whole the set of a poet's genius can be easily determined by the side to which he gravitates.

Thus, Spenser and Milton, very different from each other though they are, are essentially synthesizing poets whose instinct is to set their experiences, observations, and knowledge against a public background, to draw their diverse materials together into a great objective pattern of moral life. Donne, on the other hand, focuses even the most public themes through his personal psychology and gives them scope through the liveliness and complexity of the expression of his emotional and intellectual reactions. Tennyson operated most successfully in the world of personal plangency, his lyrical genius turning naturally to the elegiac cadence, and when, as in *In Memoriam*, he tries to sublimate personal emotion into a large public moral theme, he fails, and the poem falls apart into a series of lyrics. He failed, too, to give epic scope to his Arthurian poems, which are least successful when most obviously related to the over-all moral pattern. Indeed, few nineteenth-century poets had the epic touch, though many had epic ambitions. Whitman, however, had both the prophetic and the confessional strains in equal

degree, and is unique among poets of the English language in his combination of them. He saw himself epically; his most trivial experience
was thus potentially heroic, and his least observation could be presented
as cosmic. He does not write epics, but he cultivates an epic pose in
order to write lyrics. The result, in his more successful poems, is a remarkable counterpointing of the individual and the social, the personal
and the political, the confessional and the prophetic.

Whitman was a rhetorician and a poseur, and these are bad words
in modern criticism. But there are good and bad ways of being rhetorical, and good and bad ways of posing. In his best poetry, Whitman's
rhetoric was a device for expanding lyrical impressionism into epic
design, and his posing was a means of giving moral scope to his observations. His own introductory statement of his theme—

> One's-self I sing, a simple separate person,
> Yet utter the word Democratic, the word En-Masse—

does not represent his happiest form of expression, but it expresses an
all-important point, the desire to speak for a civilization through self-
expression. His technical problem was to find the appropriate kind of
expansive imagery, the rhetorical means of enlarging the "I" into a
grand symbolic figure, both ideal observer and epitome of all that is
observed, a benevolent god surveying his creation with infinite understanding and at the same time the suffering servant who participates
in all human woe (as well as in all human endeavor) and by participat-
ing achieves sanctification and redemption.

> I am the man, I suffer'd, I was there,

he exclaims in *Song of Myself*, reminding us of the Biblical: "In all
their affliction he was afflicted." And this is the simplest way of establishing his representative role:

> Walt Whitman, a kosmos, of Manhattan the son,
> Turbulent, fleshy, sensual, eating, drinking and breeding,
> No sentimentalist, no stander above men and women or apart
>   from them,
> No more modest than immodest. . . .

> Whoever degrades another degrades me,
> And whatever is done or said returns at last to me.

"Precisely what a kosmos is we trust Mr. Whitman will take an early
occasion to inform the impatient public," remarked Charles Eliot Norton sardonically in an article on Whitman written soon after the first

publication of *Leaves of Grass*. The answer to Norton's question is perfectly simple. A kosmos, as Whitman uses the word, is the individual human being expanded through appropriate poetic devices to be a symbolic representative of all mankind.

It has been claimed that Walt Whitman was "erethistic"; he was, says Mark Van Doren, "one of those persons whose organs and tissues are chronically in a state of abnormal excitement, who tremble and quiver when the rest of us are merely conscious that we are being interested or pleased." But what interests the critic of Whitman's poetry is the use Whitman makes of this quality in his poetry. It is used as a means of intensifying contact to the point of identification. This is clearly seen in *Song of Myself*, the poem in which Whitman strives most obviously to establish his inclusive and representative status:

> You villain touch! what are you doing? my breath is tight in
>   its throat,
> Unclench your floodgates, you are too much for me.
>
> Blind loving wrestling touch, sheath'd hooded sharp-tooth'd
>   touch!
> Did it make you ache so, leaving me?

This leads eventually to:

> I find I incorporate gneiss, coal, long-threaded moss, fruits,
>   grains, esculent roots,
> And am stucco'd with quadrupeds and birds all over,
> And have distanced what is behind me for good reasons,
> But call any thing back again when I desire it.

And this, after an interesting and well-known transitional passage about animals ("They bring me tokens of myself") and one of his great catalogues listing American activities, leads in turn to the statements of multiple identification:

> My voice is the wife's voice, the screech by the rail of the stairs,
> They fetch my man's body up dripping and drown'd. . . .
>
> I am the hounded slave, I wince at the bite of the dogs, . . .
>
> I am the mash'd fireman with breast-bone broken,
> Tumbling walls buried me in their debris, . . .
>
> I am an old artillerist, I tell of my fort's bombardment,
> I am there again.

Touch is the sense that leads to identity, and, identity once achieved, the catalogue of what the individual sees becomes an epic evocation of all American civilization. "I expected him to make the songs of the nation, but he seems content to make the inventories," remarked Emerson, retracting something of his earlier praise of Whitman. But Whitman's inventories, at their best, are epic inventories, introduced only after the poet's grand symbolic stature has been established; they can be compared with Homer's catalogue of ships and with similar devices in Milton—except, of course, that in tone and purpose they are unique and essentially Whitmanesque, vivid camera shots of a nation at work in all its variety and multiplicity, expert montage to project the picture of a civilization. Once the poet has established the stature and function of the "I" in his poem, he can achieve epic effects by lyrical methods.

Not all Whitman's devices for establishing the stature of the "I" are successful. His use of foreign, or supposedly foreign, words for this purpose is sometimes disastrous, especially in his earlier attempts. "Me imperturbe" is not a happy phrase, nor does the expression "O to be self-balanced for contingencies" express adequately the relation of self to environment which is the theme of so much of his poetry. It is not the striking phrase but the cumulative catalogue that achieves Whitman's best effects. It takes time for him to move from confession to prophecy; the process is necessarily discursive:

> I know perfectly well my own egotism,
> Know my omnivorous lines and must not write any less,
> And would fetch you whoever you are flush with myself.

> Not words of routine this song of mine,
> But abruptly to question, to leap beyond yet nearer bring;
> This printed and bound book—but the printer and the printing-office boy?
> The well-taken photograph—but your wife or friend close and solid in your arms?
> The black ship mail'd with iron, her mighty guns in her turrets—but the pluck of the captain and engineers?
> In the houses the dishes and fare and furniture—but the host and hostess, and the look out of their eyes?
> The sky up there—yet here or next door, or across the way?
> The saints and sages in history—but you yourself?
> Sermons, creeds, theology—but the fathomless human brain,
> And what is reason? and what is love? and what is life?

Whitman's characteristic procedure is to work from himself, the observer, to the observed world, through a selective catalogue of what is observed, and thence to the question, the generalization, and the prophecy. Then at once back to himself again, and the process continues.

This perpetual return to himself determines the structure of *Song of Myself*. The confession, the description, the conclusion. First, the confession, e.g.:

> I am satisfied—I see, dance, laugh, sing; . . .

Or:

> I am of old and young, of the foolish as much as the wise, . . .

Or:

> It is time to explain myself—let us stand up.

The return to self precedes the outward movement, the embrace, and as the poem proceeds observer and observed become identified, the self becomes mankind, the theme the hailing and accepting of all existence:

> Do I contradict myself?
> Very well then I contradict myself,
> (I am large, I contain multitudes.)

Whitman needed the catalogue if he was to move successfully from the lyric to the epic mood. The short, generalized poems are the least successful. In "For You O Democracy," for example, one of the lyrics in *Calamus*, he moves directly to the general statement, and the force of the poem is lost in abstractions and in unsuccessful attempts at distillation of meaning through the apt phrase rather than by means of the cumulative building up of the effect. Whitman's genius was cumulative, not epigrammatic, and that is why he failed with such a poem as "For You O Democracy":

> Come, I will make the continent indissoluble,
> I will make the most splendid race the sun ever shone upon,
> I will make divine magnetic lands,
>   With the love of comrades,
>   With the life-long love of comrades. . . .

> For you these from me, O Democracy, to serve you ma femme!
> For you, for you I am trilling these songs.

This misguided attempt at rapid general statement is followed in *Cala-mus* by an excellent example of Whitman's proper style: "These I Singing in Spring" works by building up detail, not by jumping at a generalization:

> These I singing in spring collect for lovers,
> (For who but I should understand lovers and all their sorrow and joy?
> And who but I should be the poet of comrades?)
> Collecting I traverse the garden the world, but soon I pass the gates,
> Now along the pond-side, now wading in a little, fearing not the wet,
> Now by the post-and-rail fences where the old stones thrown there, pick'd from the fields, have accumulated,
> (Wild-flowers and vines and weeds come up through the stones and partly cover them, beyond these I pass,)
> Far, far in the forest, or sauntering later in summer, before I think where I go,
> Solitary, smelling the earthy smell, stopping now and then in the silence,
> Alone I had thought, yet soon a troop gathers around me,
> Some walk by my side and some behind, and some embrace my arms or neck, . . .

This continuous moving to and fro between the poet and what he observes is a feature of nearly all Whitman's successful poems, as is the oscillation between the "I" and the "you" or the "I" and the "they":

> Alone I had thought, yet soon a troop gathers around me.

Perhaps the simplest of all Whitman's longer poems, and one which shows his characteristic method used most openly and without any complication, is *Salut au Monde!* which is organized in terms of three questions. First, "What widens within you Walt Whitman?" establishes the basic relationship between himself and what he observes and thinks of:

> What widens within you Walt Whitman?
> What waves and soils exuding?
> What climes? what persons and cities are here?
> Who are the infants, some playing, some slumbering?
> Who are the girls? who are the married women?

> Who are the groups of old men going slowly with their arms
>   about each other's necks?
> What rivers are these? what forests and fruits are these?
> What are the mountains call'd that rise so high in the mists?
> What myriads of dwellings are they fill'd with dwellers?
>
> Within me latitude widens, longitude lengthens, . . .

The first question, or complex of questions, is followed by "What do
you hear Walt Whitman?" and the answer is a typical Whitman catalogue:

> I hear the workman singing and the farmer's wife singing,
> I hear in the distance the sounds of children and of animals
>   early in the day, . . .

and so on, swelling out over the world to conclude:

> I hear the Hindoo teaching his favorite pupil the loves, wars,
>   adages, transmitted safely to this day from poets who wrote
>   three thousand years ago.

Then comes the third question:

> What do you see Walt Whitman?
> Who are they who salute, and that one after another salute you?

And the answer is again a catalogue:

> I see a great round wonder rolling through space,
> I see diminute farms, hamlets, ruins, graveyards, jails, factories,
>   palaces, hovels, huts of barbarians, tents of nomads upon
>   the surface, . . .

The vision ranges through history, geography, and mythology to end
with his identification of himself with what he sees and his salute to all:

> I see ranks, colors, barbarisms, civilizations, I go among them,
>   I mix indiscriminately,
> And I salute all the inhabitants of earth.

And then, after this counterpointing of lyrical self-expression with epic
description, the poem rises to its culminating prophetic exhortation:

> You whoever you are!
> You daughter or son of England!
> You of the mighty Slavic tribes and empires! you Russ in Rus-
>   sia!

> You dim-descended, black, divine-soul'd African, large, fine-
> headed, nobly-form'd, superbly destin'd, on equal terms
> with me!
> You Norwegian! Swede! Dane! Icelander! you Prussian!
> You Spaniard of Spain! you Portuguese! . . .

And the great catalogue swells out, to return at the end to the poet
again:

> My spirit has pass'd in compassion and determination around
> the whole earth,
> I have look'd for equals and lovers and found them ready for me
> in all lands,
> I think some divine rapport has equalized me with them. . . .
>
> Toward you all, in America's name,
> I raise high the perpendicular hand, I make the signal,
> To remain after me in sight forever,
> For all the haunts and homes of men.

Thus in Whitman the structure is of the highest importance; the
catalogues have meaning because of the intermediate place they occupy
between the poet's first announcement of himself as observer and his
final return to himself as inclusive consciousness. No poet is less quot-
able; repetition and accumulation are his methods, and a passage outside its context is likely to sound either mechanical or inflated.

Whitman's cumulative method also means that his poetry is more
open-worked than the kind of poetry which modern criticism is best
equipped to handle. Its meaning is developed lengthwise, not depth-
wise; words acquire new meaning by reiteration, and images take on
significance by functioning in a series. Sometimes Whitman seems to
be impatient of this slow process, and breaks into premature generalizations or whips the poem on with exclamations such as "Allons!" or
"Listen!" In *Song of the Open Road* (where both these exclamations
occur), he hurries on the poem by displaying himself moving through
the scenes he describes, and symbolizes his sense of identity with all
he observes by addressing the poem to a "Camerado" with whom the
journey is made. The foreign exclamations suggest an impatience with
the limitations of the English language, a desire to utter a word more
evocative and more compelling than any which his native speech can
supply, to sum up a catalogue in a slogan. It is this feature of his
work which has made so many critics see Whitman as primarily a

rhetorician, a spouter of grandiose language. But this is no essential part of his method; indeed, it is in some degree a departure from his characteristic and most successful method. The exclamation, like the generalization, is a display of impatience with the poem: Whitman sometimes can't wait for the meaning to develop cumulatively, which is his true way. In *Song of the Open Road* he introduces observations such as:

> Of the progress of the souls of men and women along the grand
> roads of the universe, all other progress is the needed emblem
> and sustenance.

This breaks the flow and sweep of the poem, and gives an effect which is merely verbose. Exclamations take their proper place at the beginning of one of the great lists, and generalizations may provide an appropriate comment or summing up at the end, but in the middle of a poem they are likely to be otiose. And even at the end, the most apt conclusion is more often a gesture ("I stop somewhere waiting for you") or a cry ("O farther, farther, farther sail!") than a reflection. How much more effective these are than the lame conclusion of *A Broadway Pageant*:

> They are justified, they are accomplish'd, they shall now be
> turn'd the other way also, to travel toward you thence,
> They shall now also march obediently eastward for your sake
> Libertad.

Where the concluding generalization is not a philosophic comment but a gathering together of the themes developed in the poem or a recapitulation in a more personal way of the dominant images of the poem, it can be at least as successful as the cry or the gesture, as is shown by the fine return which ends "When Lilacs Last in the Dooryard Bloom'd":

> Yet each to keep and all, retrievements out of the night,
> The song, the wondrous chant of the gray-brown bird,
> And the tallying chant, the echo arous'd in my soul,
> With the lustrous and drooping star with the countenance full
> of woe,
> With the holders holding my hand nearing the call of the bird,
> Comrades mine and I in the midst, and their memory ever to
> keep, for the dead I loved so well.
> For the sweetest, wisest soul of all my days and lands—and this
> for his dear sake,

> Lilac and star and bird twined with the chant of my soul,
> There in the fragrant pines and the cedars dusk and dim.

This poem stands somewhat apart from Whitman's other major works; like the others, it works through accumulation, but the movement is subtler and the images more richly patterned than in, say, *Song of Myself*, where the expansion from lyric to epic is achieved by a continuous reciprocal movement from the poet outward and from what the poet sees back to the poet. "When Lilacs Last" is at once elegy, panegyric, and manifesto, an expression of personal emotion and a public celebration, a song of woe and a song of hope. Avoiding any of the traditional modes of elegy, where devices for moving from lament to hope could be supplied either by pastoral convention or religious faith, or both, Whitman nevertheless manages to give his poem the same movement as "Lycidas" or "Adonais," the movement from grief to celebration to hope, but his method is wholly his own. First comes the clearly etched personal moment, associated at once with the two dominant images of the star and the bird. The linking of lilac, star, and bird is the linking of the poet's self to the poet's theme. The expansion here is not from lyric to epic but from personal reminiscence to public elegy. The catalogue has its place here too; what the poet sees or imagines he sees, what he hears, and what he dreams weaving together to form a rich complex of memory, grief, homage, and confidence. It is the most delicate of Whitman's major poems, using his characteristic technique in a more restrained and a more complex way than is usual with him. "Out of the Cradle Endlessly Rocking" is perhaps the closest to it in pattern and movement; both poems have shorter lines and fewer swellings out into the heavy rhetorical cadence than most of Whitman's. But "Out of the Cradle" is less subdued in tone and less subtly modulated in movement; it is punctuated at regular intervals by the exclamatory moment. Though there is apostrophe ("O powerful western fallen star!") in "When Lilacs Last," there is nothing like the "Shine! shine! shine!" or "O past! O happy life! O songs of joy!" of "Out of the Cradle," and the poem is the better for this lack.

Another interesting feature of "When Lilacs Last in the Dooryard Bloom'd" is its quiet opening. Whitman had a tendency to announce his theme before developing it:

> Come said the Muse,
> Sing me a song no poet yet has chanted,
> Sing me the universal.

This is sometimes effective enough, but when he wants to anticipate the full force of the whole poem in the opening lines (which is structurally a mistake in any case) he can produce the most disconcerting effusions:

> A Phantom gigantic superb, with stern visage accosted me,
> *Chant me the poem*, it said, *that comes from the soul of America,*
> *chant me the carol of victory,*
> *And strike up the marches of Libertad, marches more powerful*
> *yet,*
> *And sing me before you go the song of the throes of Democracy.*

He does better with the subdued autobiographical opening which prepares the way for the ensuing catalogue:

> Starting from fish-shape Paumanok where I was born, . . .

If, as we have maintained, Whitman's characteristic and most effective method is cumulative, building up the observed or imagined details until they swell out to an immense epic vision, what are we to say of his shorter, lyric poems, such as those we find in *Drum-Taps*? The answer is not simply that the longer these lyrics are the better they are, though this does seem to be true on the whole. We note also that these poems take their place in a sequence and derive much of their effect from this. "Vigil Strange I Kept on the Field One Night," for example, though it is written in the first person, reads like a moment in an epic—reminiscent, say, of Achilles' sorrowing over Patroclus in the twenty-third book of the *Iliad*: ". . . And as with a garment they covered all the body with their hair that they cut off and cast on it; and behind them great Achilles held the head, mourning; for peerless was the comrade whom he was speeding to the underworld." Whitman's tone, though so much more personal, is not dissimilar:

> Vigil for comrade swiftly slain, vigil I never forget, how as day
> brighten'd,
> I rose from the chill ground and folded my soldier well in his
> blanket,
> And buried him where he fell.

A poem like "The Wound-Dresser" is long enough to achieve by itself the characteristic Whitman sweep, but such short pieces as "Cavalry Crossing a Ford" or "Bivouac on a Mountain Side" derive their effectiveness from their place in the total sequence. Some of the poems in *Drum-Taps* are what the journalists would call "human interest" pieces, and they have indeed a journalistic aptness and interest. "Come

Up from the Fields Father" describes the receipt of a letter from a wounded soldier by his parents (the soldier is in fact already dead but the parents do not know this). It captures the moment effectively enough—

> Open the envelope quickly,
> O this is not our son's writing, yet his name is sign'd,
> O a strange hand writes for our dear son, O stricken mother's soul!

—but it is superior journalism rather than a poem. It might be an incident in a novel; but it has no epic touch, none of the Whitmanesque building up toward an inclusive vision, nor does it—unlike other of the shorter *Drum-Taps* poems—derive any new meaning from its context in the series. This kind of poem has its own appeal, but it does not represent Whitman at his most characteristic or his most impressive.

Homer and Ossian and the Bible clearly had their influence on Whitman. From the first he got the sense of epic background, the ability to see the individual in a large public context and to see him more, not less, clearly this way. From the second, he may have got suggestions for a free rhythmic prose as well as for the counterpointing of lyrical emotion with heroic design. From the third he got the accent of prophecy. But his method of combining these qualities is his own. His cumulative method, his use of the catalogue, his identification of himself with what he observes, are not easily paralleled among other poets. One might say simply that by elevating himself to heroic stature he could make an epic utterance out of a lyrical cry, and this is true enough, except that it ignores the most interesting question— how he succeeds in achieving this elevation. Perhaps his most ambitious poem, where he moves furthest from his sole self (yet without ever leaving it) to achieve an almost mystical unity with all history and geography, all human thought, all mankind, is *Passage to India*, a splendid example of his favorite method. Here he begins with himself contemplating "the strong light works of engineers," the crossing of the American continent by a continuous railroad, and the cutting of the Suez canal, and then proceeds to build up most carefully a series of opposites which it is part of the poem's function to reconcile—the Old World and the New, the East and the West, the past and the present. He sees history through geography (as Milton did, yet how differently!), and nowhere does he use the catalogue so flexibly and eloquently as in his pictures of the Oriental past and the Occidental present, seen with the voyaging eye. Yet himself as observer is never lost sight of: he reminds us by such parenthetic phrases as "(I my shores of America walking to-day behold, resuming all,)" or "(Curious in time I stand, noting the efforts of heroes, . . .)" as well as by more direct and passionate returns to himself—

> Passage indeed O soul to primal thought,
> Not lands and seas alone, thy own clear freshness, . . .

—that the poem is lyrical in mood though epic in scope. And after his visions of the beginnings of civilization, of the march of history and the challenge of the present, he sees the passage to India as ever more significant in implication, ever wider in scope, ever more symbolic of human destiny. At the end, characteristically, he simultaneously comes back to himself and expands his symbolic meaning to its utmost. This is the Whitman method operating most effectively:

> O sun and moon and all you stars! Sirius and Jupiter!
> Passage to you!

> Passage, immediate passage! the blood burns in my veins!
> Away O soul! hoist instantly the anchor!
> Cut the hawsers—haul out—shake out every sail!
> Have we not stood here like trees in the ground long enough?
> Have we not grovel'd here long enough, eating and drinking
>   like mere brutes?
> Have we not darken'd and dazed ourselves with books long
>   enough?

> Sail forth—steer for the deep waters only,
> Reckless O soul, exploring, I with thee, and thou with me,
> For we are bound where mariner has not yet dared to go,
> And we will risk the ship, ourselves and all.

> O my brave soul!
> O farther farther sail!
> O daring joy, but safe! are they not all the seas of God?
> O farther, farther, farther sail!

The excitement of these lines is not as excessive as may appear if they are read out of context. For the excitement is built up as the poem moves, and rises inevitably to this climax of both outward expansion and return to the poet's self. None of Whitman's poems repays a careful analysis of its structure more than *Passage to India*.

Of course Whitman's method was dangerous; he constantly risked verbosity and pretentiousness, and he risked, too, wearying the reader before he could get properly into the spirit and movement of the poem. His lapses are outrageous and his near misses particularly tiresome. Whitman is dangerous, too, in another way: he often seems more facile than he really is and thus encourages the view that to produce his kind of poetry you have simply to let the words splash out across the page. In fact, his poetry is not easy to imitate and, though his influence in loosening up the rhythms of poetry has been considerable on both sides of the Atlantic, there have been few successful poems written by anyone else in his style. The poetic catalogue is not an easy device to handle, nor is it a simple matter to expand lyrical emotion into epic vision through the manipulation of accumulated detail. This was Whitman's unique achievement: he created his own poetic conventions in response to his own poetic needs. In this sense he is the first truly original American poet. He wrote always as though he were the first poet, faced with the necessity of creating his own idiom and his own conception of poetry. This is perhaps a barbarian attitude—this view that solutions are to be found by examining the nature of the present case rather than by working through traditional forms. Whitman's "barbaric yawp" presented a challenge to the accepted view of the place of convention in art. But it was not uncontrolled, or merely exclamatory, or merely rhetorical. It was the idiom of a poet who had a complex vision which brought together himself, his country, and his world, thus uniting the egotist and the prophet, the patriot and the visionary, to end with a bodying forth of

> The melodious character of the earth,
> The finish beyond which philosophy cannot go and does not
>   wish to go,
> The justified mother of men.

Walt Whitman: The Prophet of Democracy

It is now nearly fifty years since my classical tutor at Oxford, H. F. Fox—whom I name, though his name will be meaningless to others, for the private satisfaction of commemorating him—pressed upon me Whitman's *Democratic Vistas*. Fox belonged to the old generation of English Liberals, who flourished in the latter decades of the nineteenth century. As a political force, they reached their apogee in the famous general election of 1906, when the Liberal party swept into power on a wave of universal reaction against the imperialist fervours of the South African war; and they were broken, permanently, by the first World War, which was undreamt of by their philosophy. But their fortunes as politicians are irrelevant. The best of the Liberals—such a one survives still in Gilbert Murray—were not politicians: they were idealists. And for one of them *Democratic Vistas* was a sort of modern bible. I imagine that this was true of many others.

They were not mistaken in saluting Whitman as their prophet. *Democratic Vistas* is surely a permanent statement, not only of the ideal of liberal democracy, but of its fundamental principles, which if it violates, it ceases to be. Democracy is a debased and ambiguous word today, when the spokesmen of totalitarian Russia make their monstrous claim that their society is a democracy, and have it granted even by some millions of Western Europeans. Therefore, I prefer to call the society which Whitman envisaged and championed the free society. But it is immaterial. There is no mistake possible about the kind of society of which Whitman was the prophet and champion.

"That which really balances and conserves the social and political world is not so much legislation, police, treaties, and dread of punishment, as the latent eternal intuitional sense in humanity, of fairness, manliness, decorum etc. Indeed this perennial regulation, control, and oversight, by self-suppliance, is *sine qua non* to democracy; and a highest, widest aim of democratic literature may well be to bring forth, cultivate, brace and strengthen this sense, in individuals and society. A strong mastership of the general inferior self by the superior self, is to be aided, secured, indirectly but surely, by the literatus, in his works, shaping for individual or aggregate democracy, a great passionate body, in and along with which goes a great masterful spirit."

That is, at once, a proclamation of Whitman's ideal of democracy, and of the part he felt that he was called to play in its realization. It is noble and compelling. And of *Democratic Vistas* in general it may be said that, apart from its own intrinsic merits, which are very great, it is necessary to an understanding of the real purpose of *Leaves of Grass*.

Yet this was the book of which Whitman wrote to Dowden in 1872 that "it remains quite unread, uncalled for, here in America." Though there is the best precedent for a prophet being without honour in his own country, in the case of Whitman it needs some explanation. The one which occurs most readily to an Englishman is that the Americans of Whitman's time were too engrossed in the material mastering of a continent to have time to pause and take their spiritual bearings, whereas the little body of contemporary and influential Englishmen, who received his work with enthusiasm, had, whether consciously or not, the premonition that the epoch of their country's expansion was over, and that if Britain was to retain significance as a power for civilization, it must be as a paradigm of the free society. Whitman made his impact upon Britain at a moment when its best minds were engaged in taking spiritual stock of their country. Carlyle, Ruskin, Arnold, and Morris were the influences which had worked on the younger men who were receptive to Whitman, and Whitman seemed to corroborate and combine those influences in a radically new way. He shifted the balance from the critical to the creative, from dubiety to faith; and he added a comprehensive assertion—a poetic demonstration—of the validity of the individual which came to his English disciples as a great liberation.

What Whitman was attempting in *Leaves of Grass* cannot be better described than he described it in *Democratic Vistas:*

"The literature, songs, esthetics etc. of a country are of importance principally because they furnish the materials and suggestions of personality for the men and women of that country, and enforce them in a thousand effective ways."

Very likely, this purpose was not fully conscious in him when he began writing *Leaves of Grass*; indeed, he admitted it. But this is what he subsequently believed he had done, or tried to do. His belief was well founded, and his claim just. This we must admit, whether or not we share his belief that a national literature is principally of importance because it offers suggestions and materials for what he elsewhere calls "a basic model or portrait of personality for general use." Even those who hold that literature has other purposes to serve, which seem to them more important, must allow that much of the world's great literature has been valued by the people for whom it was written for the concrete ideal of personal conduct it set before them. This was the merit of Homer in the eyes of a Greek, and of Virgil in the eyes of a Roman.

Such was the sense in which Whitman claimed to be the poet-prophet of America. There was nothing narrowly national in his conception of "these States." If at first sight it sometimes appears to be so, only a little patience and receptiveness are needed to make us realize that his insistence on the places, the persons, and the society with which he was familiar is only an example of the working of Goethe's poetical axiom that the universal is the particular. The universal of which "these States" were the particular in Whitman's poetry is Democracy; and all over the world democrats, in Whitman's peculiar and profound sense of the word—that is, those who believe that a self-governing society of free and responsible individuals offers the only way of progress towards the Good—have had no difficulty in regarding Whitman's America as the city of their own soul. It is for them a symbol of the ideal, of the same order as Blake's Albion and Jerusalem; and Whitman, in rhapsodizing over the rivers and prairies and people of America, is behaving as Shakespeare's poet, "who gives to airy nothing a local habitation and a name"—except that the ideal Democracy is much more than "an airy nothing." It is at least a compelling vision of the society toward which humanity must stumble on, if it is not to cease to be human.

At the present moment many Western Europeans, who have an emotional and intellectual loyalty to the ideal of the free society, are tempted to be a little dubious towards America's claim to be its prototype. To them the activities of Senator McCarthy loom large and ominous. They should remember that Whitman himself passed through many moments of despondence in the days of the carpetbaggers and afterwards. He too cried: "These savage, wolfish parties alarm me—owning no law but their own will, more and more combative, less and less tolerant of the idea of ensemble and of equal brotherhood, the perfect equality of the States, the ever overarching American ideas." Nevertheless, Whitman held to his faith that these ugly and depressing manifestations were like the grim, growing pains of the ideal, inseparable from the process of the working out of a high destiny in a mass of common humanity. Whether his faith will be justified by the event, who can say? But there is scope for tempered optimism, when we remember that, in the years immediately following Whitman's death, another idealist, of a different kidney indeed, but equally combining with his idealism a robust realism, wrote of the condition of the United States.

"Turn to Republican America. America has no Star Chamber, and no feudal barons. But it has Trusts; and it has millionaires whose factories, fenced in by live electric wires and defended by Pinkerton retainers with magazine rifles, would have made a Radical of Reginald Front de Bœuf. Would Washington or Franklin have lifted a finger in the cause of American independence if they had foreseen its reality?"

So wrote Bernard Shaw at the turn of the nineteenth century. After fifty years those conditions seem to belong to a prehistoric past, as do the conditions which produced the two epoch-making strikes—of the dockers and of the match-factory girls—in England. Democracy is at least free to mend its ways.

It is notable that Shaw, who no doubt imbibed much of his doctrine from Whitman, or rather found in Whitman a corroboration of his own native intuitions, agreed with him wholeheartedly in his insistence on the importance of sexual selection. The whole of *Man and Superman* might fairly be regarded as Shaw's effort to put a sharper and more paradoxical edge on one of Whitman's central doctrines: the necessity for Democracy of true and generous mating between mentally, morally, and physically developed men and women. Indeed, Whitman not only anticipated Shaw's doctrine of the necessity of the Superman for viable Democracy when he inveighed against "the appalling depletion of women in their powers of sane athletic maternity" and proclaimed that the radical weakness of factual society in America was that "the men believe not in the women, nor the women in the men"; but in *Children of Adam* he was the palpable forerunner of D. H. Lawrence's even more revolutionary teaching on sex. Lawrence was directly indebted to Whitman even for much of his distinctive phraseology.

This fructification in the soil of such different natures of seeds scattered from Whitman's luxuriant flowering is a simple and pertinent example of his immense seminal influence, as the poet-prophet of Democracy. That was what he justly claimed to be, and as such he is best comprehended. Or, at least, that is the best line of approach towards a complete understanding of his work: on one condition, that it is realized that Democracy can be justified and believed in only on the basis of a prior conviction of the infinite worth of the individual. Without this, Democracy is, what Plato held it to be, merely a short road to the tyranny of the baser elements in man. That can be repelled only by stubborn adherence to the sacrosanct principle of the divine right of the minority—of all minorities save one perhaps—to freedom of thought and speech. I call this right divine, because it cannot be rationally demonstrated. If it is self-evident, as I believe, it is self-evident only as a religious truth: ultimately, therefore, a matter of revelation. And since, even in the contemporary world, the truth has been categorically denied by the vast social organization of Russia, and since, in the ancient and mediaeval worlds, it was not admitted at all, it is evident that the apprehension of this religious truth is in constant need of renewal.

This was Whitman's great achievement. He vitally renewed the religious revelation on which the justification and continued existence of Democracy depends. That is to say, he experienced the revelation anew. From this derives the uniqueness of his work: the confidence with which he propounds the totality of himself—the whole experiencing nature which was Walt Whitman—as the citizen of the ideal Democracy. To the congenitally unsympathetic this has appeared as overweening arrogance, an awful example of the extravagance of romantic egotism. But no one responsive to Whitman has ever been repelled by this idiosyncrasy. It shocks only those to whom everything about Whitman is shocking. For in fact, his apparent egotism is entirely justified. It follows necessarily from his vision of the ideal society: for it is implicit in the ethos of that society that the individual shall be accepted with all his imperfections—warts and all. It is a society in which the individual person is valid, because it is a society whose law is love—the same society, in fact, of which the vision came to Tchehov when he listened to music: "where everything is forgiven and it would be strange not to forgive." In Christian idiom, it is the Kingdom of Heaven on earth. That may seem very remote from any practical democracy we know or can foresee, either in America or Europe: but the imaginative vitality of the ideal is absolutely necessary to the continuing existence of any democracy at all.

That is to say, behind and beneath Whitman's promulgation of his total self as a type of the citizen of the ideal Democracy is a deeply religious humility. Unless his "egotism" is apprehended against this background of religion it is bound to be misunderstood. Not that there is any excuse for ignoring the background. Nothing could be more explicit than, for example, *Starting from Paumanok*.

> Each is not for its own sake,
> I say the whole earth and the stars in the sky are for religion's sake.
>
> I say no man has ever yet been half devout enough,
> None has ever yet adored or worship'd half enough,
> None has begun to think how divine he himself is, and how certain the future is.
>
> I say that the real and permanent grandeur of these States must be their religion,
> Otherwise there is no real and permanent grandeur;
> (Nor character nor life worthy the name without religion,
> Nor land nor man nor woman without religion.)

It may fairly be said that Whitman's great struggle as poet-prophet was to communicate his religious sense—of the divinity of the created world, of the democratic idea; of himself as part of the one and prophet of the other—without emasculating it by using the conventional language of religion. And that, in turn, is no small part of the problem for critical appreciation of him. What we are constrained to call Whitman's humility is not very like what is ordinarily understood by the word. It is the attitude of one who has been, once for all, possessed by the conviction that he is merely the vehicle and instrument of the One, "the fang'd and glittering One whose head is over all"; who, at the same time and as part of the same experience, is convinced of the uniqueness of every created person, animal and thing; who in the words of Meister Eckhart, is as one "who having looked upon the sun, henceforward sees the sun in all things."

To be possessed by this conviction is, inevitably, felt as an immense privilege, for with it descends, also inevitably, a sense of one's total validity—no greater, indeed, than that of any blade of grass or lily of the field, but since it happens to a human being with the burden of consciousness and self-consciousness, bringing with it an incomparable awareness of integration, of liberation, and of ordinariness. To a man who has passed through this experience, egotism and humility are indistinguishable. The completest self-utterance is not an assertion but an annihilation of the self. The ego which, according to Pascal, is "always hateful," is by this experience transcended or abolished.

The proof of this, in Whitman's case, is easily available. No one who has responded to the personality exposed in *Leaves of Grass* has ever felt him to be other than lovable. One may be, indeed many are, completely allergic to him: but once he has found an entry, he takes possession, and that by a quite different process from that of conquering our aesthetic sensibilities. Not many of Whitman's poems overcome us by the perfection of their beauty; and in face of his achievement as a whole, we remain entirely aware of the crudeness, the imperfection, the failure in transmutation, of much of it. Nevertheless, we would not have it otherwise. The roughnesses, the blemishes belong. They are necessary to the kind of communication at which he aimed, and in which he believed. He well knew what he was doing when he insisted on the interdependent wholeness of the Leaves he had strung togther. When he said "the words of my book nothing, the drift of it everything," or more arrestingly, but not more profoundly, that "he who touches this book, touches a man," he was saying the same thing: that he, as a whole, had been validated.

To get to the root of this conviction, in Whitman himself and those who respond to him, we should need to inquire into the nature of the mystical experience, when it happens to a man who has worked himself free of adherence to any particular system of religion. Such an inquiry would probably not be very rewarding. It is better to accept and ponder what Whitman himself has to say of it, in the *Song of Myself.*

> I believe in you my soul, the other I am must not abase itself to you,
> And you must not be abased to the other.
>
> Loafe with me on the grass, loose the stop from your throat,
> Not words, not music or rhyme I want, not custom or lecture, not even the best,
> Only the lull I like, the hum of your valvèd voice.
>
> I mind how once we lay such a transparent summer morning,
> How you settled your head athwart my hips and gently turn'd over upon me,
> And parted the shirt from my bosom-bone, and plunged your tongue to my bare-stript heart,
> And reach'd till you felt my beard, and reach'd till you held my feet.

> Swiftly arose and spread around me the peace and knowledge
> that pass all the argument of the earth,
> And I know that the hand of God is the promise of my own,
> And I know that the spirit of God is the brother of my own,
> And that all the men ever born are also my brothers, and the
> women my sisters and lovers,
> And that a kelson of the creation is love,
> And limitless are leaves stiff or drooping in the fields,
> And brown ants in the little wells beneath them,
> And mossy scabs of the worm fence, heap'd stones, elder, mul-
> lein and poke-weed.

That seems to be a description of an actual moment of illumination,
perhaps *the* moment. By its curious and impressive particularity it
recalls nothing so much as some equally particular and impressive
passages in Blake's prophetic books. What is peculiar to Whitman is
the intensity of his physical memory of the process (which other mystics have described) by which his corporal body was, as it were, con-
sumed and spiritualized. He describes it, vividly and memorably, as
a physical caress of his body by his soul; and this swift and sudden
transcending of the distinction and opposition between body and soul
is accompanied by a vision of the infinite significance of the details of
the created world—what Blake called the Minute Particulars—and a
simultaneous assurance that "a kelson of the creation is love."
One may guess that this experience is the creative kernel of the
whole of the *Song of Myself*: the seed of which that great poem is an
exfoliation, though of course there is no way of proving it. Anyhow,
it is certain that only in the perspective established by an experience
such as he describes can the apparent contradictions of the poem be
naturally resolved and seen as necessary. If the experience is not the
originating germ of the poem, it is the key to it. And at no point in
the amazingly rich variety of its validations does Whitman go beyond
what is warranted by his mystical assurance that everything everywhere is good and divinely appointed: himself, in all his thoughts, emotions and acts, no more and no less than any other particle of the
universe. The self that he "promulges" is the self that he has discovered
at the point of its unity with the All; it is beneath anything that we are
accustomed to regard as personality. He has been carried back to the
ground of the personal (in the metaphysical sense of the word
"ground") and has found it to be of one eternal substance with every-

thing that is, or has been, or will be. This is the firm and timeless foundation from which he vaticinates.

Quite obviously, the *Song of Myself* is just as much, if not more preponderantly, the song of Whitman's not-Self, of all the richness of the objective world. Its "egotism" is transparent and crystalline : it is completely acknowledged, and in no way apologized for—

> I know perfectly well my own egotism,
> Know my omnivorous lines and must not write any less,
> And would fetch you whoever you are flush with myself.

"Flush with myself" is one of those simple and superb phrases which Whitman always had at his command. It means not merely bringing his comrade-reader to the point where he shares Whitman's perception, but bringing them both together to coalesce in a common spiritual ether. He expresses this in a splendid and homely metaphor (which may not be recognized as a metaphor) at the beginning of his *Song*.

> Houses and rooms are full of perfumes, the shelves are crowded
>   with perfumes,
> I breathe the fragrance myself and know it and like it,
> The distillation would intoxicate me also, but I shall not let it.
>
> The atmosphere is not a perfume, it has no taste of the distilla-
>   tion, it is odorless,
> It is for my mouth forever, I am in love with it,
> I will go to the bank by the wood and become undisguised and
>   naked,
> I am mad for it to be in contact with me.

That is not, what it seems, a paean to the open air ; it celebrates what Blake called "the cleansing of the doors of perception," and the entry into the new and ever-present world of things as they are. Whitman calls "the atmosphere" what Spinoza calls the *species aeternitatis*, and more traditionally Christian mystics the all-sustaining love of God. And so Whitman ends what is in deceptive appearance an invocation of the open air with a plain declaration of his real meaning.

> Have you reckon'd a thousand acres much? have you reckon'd
>   the earth much?
> Have you practis'd so long to learn to read?
> Have you felt so proud to get at the meaning of poems?

> Stop this day and night with me and you shall possess the origin
> of all poems,
>
> You shall possess the good of the earth and sun, (there are mil-
> lions of suns left,)
>
> You shall no longer take things at second or third hand, nor
> look through the eyes of the dead, nor feed on the spectres
> in books,
>
> You shall not look through my eyes either, nor take things from
> me,
>
> You shall listen to all sides and filter them from yourself.

To be intoxicated by the perfume and the distillation which he loves, but puts aside for the pure serene of "the atmosphere," is the same as looking through the eyes of the dead. It is not enough to call the condition at which he aims for himself, and which he seeks to induce in us, freshness of vision, though no doubt where that occurs a momentary transparence has taken place. He is urging us towards not a mere "moment of vision" but to an understanding of all that it involves: towards making the religion that underlies all such moments a permanent possession. The *Song of Myself* is crowded to overflowing not only with moments of vision but also with a rich multiplicity of statements and explorations of the background from which it arises. His focus changes incessantly. At one moment, impersonal as "the atmosphere," his "omnivorous lines" roam over all America; at another they pass up and down the vistas of "the Me myself," who no less belongs to all men.

The range of this great poem is wonderful: from the picture of the negro dray driver—

> The negro holds firmly the reins of his four horses, the block
> swags underneath on its tied-over chain,
>
> The negro that drives the long dray of the stone-yard, steady
> and tall he stands pois'd on one leg on the string-piece,
>
> His blue shirt exposes his ample neck and breast and loosens
> over his hip-band,
>
> His glance is calm and commanding, he tosses the slouch of his
> hat away from his forehead,
>
> The sun falls on his crispy hair and mustache, falls on the black
> of his polish'd and perfect limbs.

to "the mechanic's wife with her babe at her nipple interceding for every person born." That sudden identification of the mechanic's wife with the Blessed Virgin is of the essence of Whitman's thought.

Thus, the *Song of Myself*, rightly considered, is the explication of an eternal moment. If one is required to choose, this must be pronounced Whitman's greatest poem, and certainly the one around which all the other leaves of grass—the obviously beautiful and the apparently ungainly—naturally cluster themselves. It is the heart and core of the total pattern. The only poem I know with which it can be compared is Blake's *Milton,* which is also the explication of an eternal moment. There is one salient difference between them. Blake's wonderful poem is an exploration, or re-creation of the timeless instant itself, whereas Whitman's equally wonderful one is a declaration of its consequences. But *Milton* is barred from the common understanding by Blake's use of his esoteric symbols, where Whitman intently addressed himself, as far as he could, to the comprehension of the common man. But, for all that, the affinities between the two poems are astonishing. How perfectly, one feels, would such a passage as this from *Milton* fall into place in the *Song of Myself*!

> Thou seest the Constellations in the deep and wondrous Night:
> They rise in order and continue their immortal courses
> Upon the mountains and in vales with harp and heavenly song,
> With flute and clarion, with cups and measures fill'd with foaming wine.
> Glitt'ring the streams reflect the Vision of beatitude,
> And the calm Ocean joys beneath and smooths his awful waves:
> These are the Sons of Los, and these the Labourers of the Vintage.
>
> Thou seest the gorgeous clothed Flies that dance and sport in summer
> Upon the sunny brooks and meadows: every one the dance
> Knows in its intricate mazes of delight artful to weave:
> Each one to sound his instruments of music in the dance,
> To touch each other and recede, to cross and change and return:
> These are the Children of Los; thou seest the Trees on mountains,
> The wind blows heavy, loud they thunder thro' the darksom sky,
> Uttering prophecies and speaking instructive words to the sons
> Of men: These are the Sons of Los: These the Visions of Eternity,
> But we see only as it were the hem of their garments

When with our vegetable eyes we view these wondrous
Visions.

Save for the repeated phrase which belongs to Blake's particular drama
of the spirit, it might well be one of Whitman's canticles. And Blake
is saying precisely the same as Whitman when he declares that he
knows that

> . . . limitless are leaves stiff and drooping in the fields
> And brown ants in the little wells beneath them . . .

"Limitless" because they are visions of eternity, in Blake's language,
and we see only the hem of their garments.

It is in accord with the deeper harmony of things that Anne Gilchrist—who devoted the first years of her widowhood to completing
her husband's *Life of William Blake*, the first book in which his extraordinary genius was vindicated—should have been the first woman
publicly to salute the kindred genius of Whitman; by endorsing his
radical utterances on sex (essentially the same as Blake's), she gave
him perhaps the most precious support he ever received—"the proudest word that ever came to me from a woman—if not the proudest word
of all from any source," as he told Traubel.

Perhaps paradoxically, but rightly, Whitman believed that the immediate apprehension of an infinite significance in all existences was
within the natural capacity of the common man. The truths he enunciated were self-evident to the natural vision, though he was constrained
in honesty to admit that natural vision was not very common, since it
required the removal of the scales of custom and prejudice—indeed of
most of what was reckoned respectable.

> Long enough have you dream'd contemptible dreams,
> Now I wash the gum from your eyes . . .

Still, he insisted on the ordinariness of his own vision.

> (Only what proves itself to every man and woman is so,
> Only what nobody denies is so.)

Behind this simple asseveration is the justified assumption that, if
Democracy is not a sham, a merely temporary form of social organization, produced by a favourable conjunction of circumstances but
doomed to collapse under the pressure of any positive demands on its
assumed morality, then there must be latent in its citizens a real fund
of common and unshakable religious conviction. Every member, or at

least the majority of its members, must be deeply persuaded of the infinite worth of others as well as himself. This axiomatic moral and religious truth may be overlaid, obscured, and forgotten, but it must be there, or Democracy is an illusion. Whitman could not admit that it was, any more than I can. The most he could do was to admit the possibility that men might make the great refusal.

> Once unquestioning obedience, once fully enslaved,
> Once fully enslaved, no nation, state, city of this earth, ever
>   afterward resumes its liberty.

But he had to make the act of faith in his fellows. The revelation that had come to him was latent in them. He was merely their spokesman, the interpreter of themselves to themselves.

> I do not say these things for a dollar or to fill up the time while
>   I wait for a boat,
> (It is you talking just as much as myself, I act as the tongue
>   of you,
> Tied in your mouth, in mine it begins to be loosen'd.)

And this is true, not merely of the great democratic commonplaces to which they might be expected to respond, but of the comprehensive religious realization on which alone they can be grounded.

> (The moth and the fish-eggs are in their place,
> The bright suns I see and the dark suns I cannot see are in their
>   place,
> The palpable is in its place and the impalpable is in its place.)

> These are really the thoughts of all men in all ages and lands,
>   they are not original with me,
> If they are not yours as much as mine they are nothing, or next
>   to nothing . . .

It is indeed the *philosophia perennis* which he proclaims, but with the radical variation that he proclaims it to a society which is, or claims to be, based on the belief that all its members are at least capable of it. To them he says: Have the courage of yourselves, first by discovering what your self really is. Get down to the bedrock, the point at which you know your own infinitude, stretching forward and backward in time, and upwards to eternity. From that security go your way, fulfill your own unique destiny.

> I have no chair, no church, no philosophy,
> I lead no man to a dinner-table, library, exchange,

But each man and each woman of you I lead upon a knoll,
My left hand hooking you around the waist,
My right hand pointing to landscapes of continents and the
public road.

Not I, not anyone else can travel that road for you,
You must travel it for yourself.

It is not far, it is within reach,
Perhaps you have been on it since you were born and did not
know,
Perhaps it is everywhere on water and on land.

Whitman's hope that ordinary men and women would straightway
receive his utterances as the expression of their own deepest, but in-
articulate, thoughts and feelings, was not realized in fact. He may have
found a few such readers, but for the most part he had to depend on a
few doughty defenders in his own country—Emerson supreme among
them—and the enthusiastic support of a band of young English disciples. Indeed, writing as late as 1904, Henry Bryan Binns, his English biographer, speaking of Whitman's dismissal in 1865 from his
clerkship in the Indian Bureau in Washington, as the result of the
reading of *Leaves of Grass* by his Methodist chief, says: "Average
American opinion was then undisguisedly hostile, as, of course, it still
remains." If that was really the situation in America in 1904, it was
distinctly different from that in England, where by that time his book
had been accepted as a classic by the Liberal intellectuals, and as a sort
of bible by the native British Socialist movement, which, though it
had a fair sprinkling of intellectuals, had a solid working-class core.
Perhaps the explanation of this discrepancy is that quite early in the
nineteenth century the British working class had become more or less
completely urbanized, and Whitman's poetry had, for that part of it
which was sufficiently alert to become Socialist, a powerful nostalgic
attraction as a poetry of the open country and the open air. And it is
very probable that the curious, but very marked association of the early
Socialist movement in England with camping and hiking, on foot or
cycle, in the countryside is almost entirely due to the influence of
Whitman.

But that topic, though interesting, belongs to British local history.
It would appear, from what I have read, that it was as a person rather
than as a poet that Whitman came closest to the common man in America—pre-eminently during his hospital experiences in Washington in

the Civil War, which made so profound an impression upon him. It has been said that Whitman attributed to his war experiences a significance for his literary development which they did not really possess. This is true, in the sense that the greater part of his most characteristic work was written before the war. Nevertheless, Whitman was not mistaken about himself. The war experience did deepen his understanding of his own poetic purposes; it intensely sharpened his sense of the appalling cost even of the partial realization of the democratic ideal; it summoned him to make his own faith stronger in that which endures beyond death. That involved no break in his development, no such catastrophic change as, for example, was enforced upon the consciousness of many Englishmen by their experiences of the first World War. Whitman's faith was as deeply grounded as any could be. There is at least one passage in the *Song of Myself* in which he deliberately compares himself with the crucified and resurrected Christ. It was a brave thing to do, but in its splendid context it provokes no resistance.

> Enough! enough! enough!
> Somehow I have been stunn'd. Stand back!
> Give me a little time beyond my cuff'd head, slumbers, dreams, gaping,
> I discover myself on the verge of a usual mistake.
>
> That I could forget the mockers and insults!
> That I could forget the trickling tears and the blows of the bludgeons and hammers!
> That I could look with a separate look on my own crucifixion and bloody crowning.
>
> I remember now,
> I resume the overstaid fraction,
> The grave of rock multiplies what has been confided to it, or to any graves,
> Corpses rise, gashes heal, fastenings roll from me.
>
> I troop forth replenish'd with supreme power, one of an average unending procession,
> Inland and sea-coast we go, and pass all boundary lines,
> Our swift ordinances on their way over the whole earth,
> The blossoms we wear in our hats the growth of thousands of years.

This, again, can be paralleled in the writings of Blake, for whom the unity of all humanity is typified in "the Divine Humanity, the One Man, even Jesus," whose sufferings must be renewed in the ascent of any single soul towards Eternity. I recall Whitman's words here only to show that there was already that in him which could endure his Civil War experiences without dismay, though receiving them with the full sensitivity of the sympathetic and compassionate imagination. He saw many Christs in the agonizing soldiers he tended.

It was wholly natural, therefore, that his participation in their heroic sacrifice should deepen his conception of the Democracy for which they died, and that he should declare that "Only the occurrence of the Secession War, and what it show'd me as by flashes of light with the emotional depths it sounded and arous'd . . . that only from the strong flare and provocations of that war's sights and scenes the final reasons-for-being of an autochthonic and passionate song finally came forth." At any rate it seems to me that from this point onward, Whitman understood his purpose more clearly as that of the poet-prophet of a society to be actually realized, as it had actually been paid for in limitless human suffering. He had the satisfaction of knowing that he too had paid the price. The immense demands of the hospital years in Washington on his vital energy were the cause of his paralysis, and of the relative poverty of his subsequent poetic output.

To compensate, there is the admirable vaticination of *Democratic Vistas.* The vision and argument of this book, more directly than any of the poetry in *Leaves of Grass,* arise from his war experience. This, he seems to say, is the society of which that manifest heroism of the common man offers the earnest.

"The movements of the late secession war, and their results, to any sense that studies well and comprehends them, show that popular democracy, whatever its faults and dangers, practically justifies itself beyond the proudest claims and wildest hopes of its enthusiasts."

We who have lived to see much the same common men fight with no less heroism and endure no less suffering in defence of a system as remote from democracy as the communism of Stalin's Russia or the National Socialism of Hitler's Germany, may be a little more dubious of the validity of this demonstration. But it seemed cogent to Whitman, and perhaps he was right. And there is no doubt at all that he was right in his vindication of the Democracy he envisioned as the only form of society which can claim the moral allegiance of the free man.

"The purpose of democracy . . . is, through many transmigrations and amid endless ridicules, arguments, and ostensible failures, to illustrate, at all hazards, this doctrine or theory that man, properly trained in highest, sanest freedom, may and must become a law, and series of laws, unto himself, surrounding and providing for, not only his own personal control, but his relations to all other individuals and to the State; and that while other theories, as in the past histories of nations, have proved wise enough, and indispensable perhaps for their conditions, *this*, as matters now stand in our civilised world is the only scheme worth working from, as warranting results like Nature's laws, reliable, when once established, to carry on of themselves."

So much, nowadays, we would all claim to see and admit; but, it is to be feared, for the most part with a kind of lip service and formal adhesion. It was Whitman's greatness that he explored and promulgated all the tremendous assumptions or obligations involved in that comforting creed. During the eighty years that have followed the writing of *Democratic Vistas*, in spite of the fact that we have endured two wars, even more atrocious than the Civil War which served to open yet wider Whitman's wide-open eyes, and that these wars were fought, not only ostensibly but really, to maintain Democracy, we seem to have got no further in the way of understanding and conceiving and imagining Democracy, than to suppose it is achieved and realized in the establishment of adult suffrage for men and women. That is concrete, we seem to say, and comprehensible; that is the universal yardstick, by applying which we know whether or not Democracy exists. But beyond that, everything is vague and shadowy, uncertain and insecure. Do we recognize as essential to Democracy the divine right of a minority to freedom of thought and expression and association? We hardly know. Do we declare, as essential to Democracy, that this right must be denied to a minority which seeks to undermine and overthrow and abolish even that divine right of a minority in which we vaguely believe? We hardly know. The truth is, that once the obvious, elementary, and mechanical condition of Democracy has been satisfied in universal suffrage, perplexity involves the urgent question: what are the further fundamental moral postulates of Democracy, even on the overtly political plane? It is as though the wind of inspiration had dropped, and the proud ship drifted becalmed. She has not even steerageway.

Granted that some of the problems with which Democracy is now confronted belong to a dimension of which Whitman had no inkling, it remains true that he alone faithfully and passionately explored the hidden moral and religious bases of Democracy from which alone an answer to all its new problems can hopefully be sought. And the main substance of his discovery is that Democracy can be secured only on the foundation of its own appropriate and necessary religion. The notion of a new religion tends, perhaps justly, to be suspect. But Whitman meant no more, but no less, than that: just as Democracy can only be understood as a growth out of former organizations of society, yet must be recognized as something entirely new, so its necessary religion will incorporate and transmute all that is valid in the religions of the societies which preceded it.

> My faith is the greatest of faiths and the least of faiths,
> Enclosing worship ancient and modern and all between ancient
>   and modern.

Thus, in *Democratic Vistas*, he begins by explicitly declaring that Democracy is the development in the further field of social organization and material opportunity of the message of Christ that the nature of the individual soul is so transcendent that it sets all men on a common level. Democracy is the implementation of the equality of souls proclaimed by the founder of Christianity. But what is the soul? Whitman has no doubt at all that a soul distinct from the body is an illusion. Body and soul are one, not two. And whether we like it or not, it seems plain that this is the fundamental religious postulate of Democracy, however unsuspected it may be.

That, says Whitman anyhow, is what we discover when as free individuals we explore the reality of what we are. We find an ultimate and indefeasible unity in ourselves of soul and body: an individual One, which at the moment of its awareness of itself, is known to be part of the universal One. Thus that infinite worth and uniqueness of the individual, on which Democracy purports to be grounded, is a reality only when it is pursued to its religious recesses in an ultimate and immediate self-knowledge of what he calls "the identified soul." It is notable how close Whitman quite independently comes at this point to the language and ideas of Keats in his famous letter on the world as "The Vale of Soul-making." The following crucial declaration of Whitman's might be incorporated bodily into Keats's letter, without alteration and without perceptible discrepancy.

"Religion, although casually arrested, and, after a fashion preserved in the churches and creeds, does not depend at all on them, but is a part of the identified soul, which, when greatest, knows not bibles in the old way, but in new ways—the identified soul, which can really confront Religion when it extricates itself entirely from the churches, and not before."

So close is the resemblance between Whitman's and Keats's thought here that Keats supplies a better gloss than does Whitman himself on his key phrase, "the identified soul." For this is exactly what Keats meant when he distinguished a Soul from an Intelligence. "There may be intelligences or sparks of the divinity in millions—but they are not Souls till they acquire identities, till each one is personally itself."

This religious-ethical realization, says Whitman, is the true basis of Democracy; for it is at this point, and at this point only, that the individual becomes a reality. Short of this point, he is an illusion, on which nothing solid or durable can be built. Hence the transcendent importance for enduring Democracy of the emergence of prophets of true "personalism," as he calls it. This promulgation of "the religious element which is, finally, at the core of Democracy" is the work of the poet-prophet, the distinctive literatus of Democracy. He will work, just as the poet-prophets of former ages and former modes of society, by creating a compulsive image of the concrete, unified personality which is now required, with all its particular and essentially new emotional aptitudes and ethical and religious axioms. Of such poet-prophets of Democracy Whitman claims to be a forerunner, but no more. He is, as it were, the warning and encouraging voice of the interregnum, while Democracy is still unaware of the need of imaginative patterns adequate to its own unconscious assumptions and potentialities—and dangers. The dangers he sees clearly—most apprehensively in "the long series of tendencies, shapings, which few are strong enough to resist, and which now seem, with steam-engine speed, to be everywhere turning out the generations of humanity like uniform iron castings."

"All of which, as compared with the feudal ages, we can yet do nothing better than accept, make the best of, and even welcome, upon the whole for their oceanic practical grandeur, and their restless wholesale kneading of the masses—I say of all this tremendous and dominant play of solely materialistic bearings upon current life in the United States, with the results as already seen, accumulating, and reaching far into the future, that they must either be confronted and met by at least an equally subtle and tremendous force-infusion for purposes of spiritualisation, for the pure conscience, for genuine aesthetics, and for absolute and primal manliness or womanliness—or else our modern civilisation, with all its improvements, is in vain, and we are on the road to a destiny, a status, equivalent in its real world, to that of the fabled damned."

The process of spiritualization which alone can save Democracy from moral disaster Whitman here defines as consisting in three things. First, the awakening of the pure conscience, which is, of course, not pure in the puritan sense, because it includes a candid and delighted recognition of all the mysteries of sex—a recognition inseparable from the knowledge of our participation in and dependence upon the infinite. This knowledge is the immediate source of the pure conscience, because it binds us, with a new sense of obligation, both to the One and to our fellow men. It is in the discovery of a new and deeper meaning in the Christian summons that we shall become, by knowing ourselves to be, "sons of God." Second, the establishment of absolute and primal womanliness and manliness: the condition in which "the men believe in the women and the women in the men." By which he means the creation of a bond of true love between them, whereby they entirely trust each other: which involves, above all, for Whitman, as for Blake before him, the abolition of sexual secrecy. Man and woman recognize, revere, and delight in each other as palpable manifestations of the divine. They acknowledge their several and mutual dependence upon the infinite, each with his own sense of responsibility. Third, there is genuine aesthetics—the establishment of an ideal and image of attainable beauty, moral and physical, in the common consciousness which will attract the aspirations of men and women, and serve them as a criterion to judge themselves and others: an image and ideal corresponding to the καλὸς κἀγαθός of the Greeks, the *vir pietate gravis* of the Romans, the *honnête homme* of seventeenth-century France, or the Christian gentleman of English-speaking peoples. But these were ideals evolved in and appropriate to aristocratic societies, and almost exclusively masculine. The new ideal image must be consubstantial with the new society, in which men and women are equals and lovers, and men and men comrades; it must arise from and be prophetic of Democracy "which alone," Whitman says magnificently, "on anything like Nature's scale, breaks up the limitless fallows of humankind and plants the seeds of personalism."

In this sense Whitman conceived himself as a poet-prophet co-operating with the silent workings of Democracy, and making communication to the responsive among its members of an image of the new democratic man. Yet image-making, though it was his chosen phrase, and indeed the best he could use to describe his purpose, is inadequate to what he tried to do, and did. He made a total communication of himself. His work was at once less and more than a poetic achievement. There is splendid and immortal poetry in it: perfectly formed and crystalline gems in the mass of ore. But they, without the matrix which surrounds them, would lose the greater part of their significance. And, indeed, we need them less for what they are in themselves than as the immediate and indisputable evidence that in Whitman was a truly great poet, judged by the most conservative standards. But the matrix is more important than the gems; the total Whitman far more dynamic, far more charged with potential for humanity, than his rounded utterances. The Whitman who gropes his way from the basis of his deep and new-discovered personality, his identified soul, into the vast variety of his incomplete affirmations; who offers himself with all his hesitations, his contradictions, and his deep unformulable faith, to his comrades of the future is a truly prophetic man. He is, in part, the attractive image of the citizen of the new completely human society of which the crude integument is what we call Democracy; he is, in a yet more important part, the tongue-tied soul in travail of the idea of which he is the instinctive vehicle. And this part of him, which is quite inseparable from the other, is perhaps even more durable than the image of the rounded man which he communicates. For it is inherent in this conception of Democracy, as the constant, endless breaking of the fallows of humankind for the sowing of the seed of personality, that it should never reach finality. The process is as recurrent and illimitable as the labours of the veritable husbandry of the earth. Seedtime and harvest, the quiescence of winter frost, the saving and selection of new seed, the ploughing and the fight against the weeds—

> These shall go onward the same
> Though dynasties pass.

So with the process of Democracy. Its faith will never be finally uttered; the final utterances will always be of faiths not its own. The image of its citizen will never be completed. Always there will be the need, to urge it onward, of that sacred and consecrated band of brothers of which Whitman dreamed.

"Yet I have dreamed, merged in that hidden-tangled problem of our fate, whose long unravelling stretches mysteriously through time— dreamed out, portrayed, hinted already—a little or a larger band—a band of brave and true, unprecedented yet—armed and equipped at every point—the members separated, it may be, by different dates and States, or south, or north, or east, or west—Pacific, Atlantic, Southern, Canadian—a year, a century here, and other centuries there—but always one, compact in soul, conscience-conserving, God-inculcating, inspired achievers, not only in literature, the greatest art, but achievers in all art—a new, undying order, dynasty, from age to age transmitted—a band, a class, at least as fit to cope with current years, our dangers, needs, as those who, for their times, so long, so well, in armour or in cowl, upheld and made illustrious, that far-back feudal, priestly world. To offset chivalry, indeed, those vanished countless knights, old altars, abbeys, priests, ages and strings of ages, a knightlier and more sacred cause today demands, and shall supply, in a New World, to larger, grander work, more than the counterpart and tally of them."

Whitman the incomplete, sustained by the inward knowledge that his own sincerely acknowledged and avowed incompleteness would make him forever contemporary with the pioneers of responsible personality on whom the vitality, and even the continued bare existence of the new and experimental society of Democracy will ultimately depend, is he who deserves our deepest homage. This is the man who retains, and will increase, his power to stir the thoughts of men in their dumb cradles. The compulsiveness of his certainty that the person is real only in the measure of his felt and known obligation to higher powers with which he can have immediate contact; his abiding sense of the transparent miracle of personal identity—"miracle of miracles, beyond statement, most spiritual and vaguest of earth's dreams, yet hardest basic fact, and only entrance to all facts"—his refusal to push the mystery away from the field of immediate experience, by interposing the apparatus of conventional theologies; his brave and humble confidence that "the last best dependence is to be on humanity itself, and its own normal full-grown qualities, without any superstitious support whatsoever"; his serene assurance that only this gradual, tentative, exploring attitude applied to the whole—not an arbitrary part—of a man's experience is adequately and fully religious, and that "faith, very old, now scared away by science, must be restored, brought back, by the same power that caused her departure—restored with new sway, deeper, wider, higher than ever"—these are some of the crystallizations from the marvellous and harmonious flux of creative intuitions which Whitman has conveyed to us with all the richness of their matrix of experience. "My opinions," he said gently to Traubel, "are all, always, so hazy . . . though, to be sure, when they come, they come firm." Both statements are true; but one is often neglected. Whitman's opinions are firmer and more durable than is easily believed.

INDEX

INDEX

6

APR

REC